# TELL ME NO LIES

BRIZVEGAS BILLIONAIRES BOOK 1

FIONA M MARSDEN

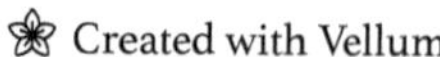 Created with Vellum

*With thanks to author Wendy Marcus,*
*Amy Andrews of Word Witchery,*
*Also the anonymous judges of RWAus*
*All of whom gave their time and expertise to make this a better*
*story.*

1

___

"*I* was promised a geek, Jimmie. Why haven't they delivered?"

The young receptionist smirked in response. "Maybe they were all out of stock."

"Oh, very funny." Harriet jabbed at the keyboard, but the screen didn't respond. "We can't do a thing until the system is back on-line. If the newsletters don't go out, next month's fundraising program will be impacted. Not in a good way."

She squirmed in her chair, unaccountably restless. Releasing a puff of air from the corner of her mouth to shift an annoying strand of hair, she keyed in the command to shut it down one more time. She could do this. She'd been doing it for years even though being the computer tech wasn't really part of her PR duties.

Resting her hands on the edge of the desk she breathed in slowly, then out. Keep calm and...*oh, bollocks*. Now she sounded like one of those stupid internet memes.

Jimmie leaned over the desk, his lank, black hair falling around his thin face. He was a good kid, always ready to see the best in any situation. She couldn't remember if she'd been the same at his age. But so much had changed for her at eighteen. Nearly seven years.

Shaking her head, she pulled her wayward thoughts back to what the boy was saying. "Gary said the computer people should be here any time. Apparently, the guy had to go to the U. S. at the last minute for some big government agency and we dropped off the radar."

She smiled up at him with a cynical twist. "As always, the non-paying charities slip to the bottom of the pile when it comes to service. If this company decide to upgrade the whole network, it would make an enormous difference. We just don't have the money to do it ourselves. Donations are down again this month. Too many charities competing, and client services are our priority."

"I don't think it was like that. I heard Gary say their head honcho rang up personally from the United States to apologise but he had no one else to send. They said he likes to keep a close eye on these projects." He grinned. "Maybe you'll get your geek after all."

Three hours later Harriet gave up, shutting down the system. She'd have to pull it apart to see if something was loose. Usually she enjoyed delving around in the guts of a computer. But today...not so much. Maybe it was all the talk about computer geeks. Bringing back other memories she preferred to keep locked away.

Memories of another time when she'd watched someone else probing the mysteries, his normally shy stammer smoothing out as he expounded on what he was doing, forgetting she was a girl. His girl.

Hunching her shoulders, she stared at the blank screen. Today hadn't been any different to the last gazillion days since she started working at LearnAble's headquarters. Coming up two years, ever since graduating with her degree in marketing. It was a challenge she relished, working to raise the profile of the small community organisation.

Adults with a disability didn't have the same cuteness factor as children and people without experience often didn't know how to relate to an adult with an intellectual impairment. Finding employment for the clients as trainees in local businesses, even with a support worker, required a lot of public education and promotion but she'd found it deeply satisfying working with the team here.

So why this restlessness? Why this edgy feeling, like a storm might break at any moment? A glance out the window showed nothing but clear skies and the tall buildings of the city centre. The bright purple of the ancient Jacaranda trees growing in the front of the building fringed the bottom of the second-floor windows.

Springtime in Brisbane. *No, not going there.* She'd promised herself, promised her parents, not to let herself wallow in regrets, the might have been. She'd already cost them so much. Had failed them in the one most important thing. Sucking in a breath she picked up the screwdriver, instructing Jimmy how to move the CPU up onto the desktop. *No...regrets...ever.*

Losing a wife was easier than finding one. Lucas Hall hadn't thought about the logistics when he'd left her behind seven years ago. He'd assumed finding her would be simple. If it ever became necessary. Knowing how to find people was part of his skillset. People didn't fall off the grid these days. They were more likely to be diving in through social media and the numerous other ways an individual could leave a digital footprint.

It had taken a year for a viable Harriet Emerson to show up, right under his nose, on an application for funding for an insignificant charitable organisation. He'd been looking in all the wrong places. Neither had he been trying very hard. He could have left it to the lawyers but for some idiotic reason, he wanted to see her first, before putting things in motion. Probably should have left it to the lawyers.

When the name popped up on his screen, his heart had given an unwelcome thump. Lucas couldn't be sure it was his Harriet, but statistically, with such an old-fashioned name, the combination with the surname, it was highly probable. *His Harriet.* Had she ever been that?

Glancing around LearnAble's chaotic reception area there was no mistaking the purpose of the organisation. Much of the clutter was equipment for people with a disability. Shelves were stacked with a jumble of books, boxes with medical illustrations and computer software. On the walls were posters advertising services and over by the reception desk a wheelchair and several bathroom aids took up space.

He recognised some of them from his mother's recent illness, before she went into the nursing home. She'd loved Harriet. Which only went to show what a good actress his ex was. Or his mother's snobbishness.

Somehow it was hard to imagine the haughty girl he remembered from their last meeting in this environment. The girl she'd pretended to be maybe. Intelligent, loving, sweet as his grandmother's cannoli. But that girl had been an illusion. Sometimes he wished he'd never had to know the truth. The lie had been...perfect.

He couldn't help smiling at the young man who seemed eager as a puppy to welcome his team. The lanky youngster looked like he might burst with excitement, but Gary Dean, the CEO, quelled him.

"Thanks, Jimmie, you can go now."

Jimmie's head dropped, and he scurried across the room to hover by the reception desk. Lucas watched him go curiously.

The prospectus said LearnAble assisted young adults with a disability to transition into work and social spheres, but it wasn't until the lad reacted to his boss's reprimand that he considered the young receptionist might also have a disability.

Lucas introduced the beaming Gary to his team and stood listening with half an ear to the man's eulogising. He'd heard it all before, but he preferred the satisfaction of a job well done to the kind of plaudits the man seemed to think were acceptable. He was here to replace the organisation's ageing computer network as part of his company's charitable arm and maybe find someone he'd been searching for since his arrival back in the country.

Gary seemed to think it necessary to give everyone a blow-by-blow of Lucas' entire career. All seven years of it. At least he hadn't delved into his university and school years. No, he'd done that too, bringing up the awards won and the scholarship to UCLA for his doctorate. Once Lucas would have curled into a ball of embarrassment, but he'd learned to let it go over his head, keeping a polite smile on his face.

Jimmie still hovered, and Lucas watched him lean over the counter to talk to someone out of sight. A low voice responded, and he glimpsed blonde hair as the speaker raised her head above the curved barrier at the front of the desk. Everything else faded as he focused on the conversation, trying to identify the female voice.

"Mr. Hall?"

Lucas turned back to the CEO. "I'm sorry, you were saying?"

"We don't have a tech person on staff, unfortunately. Our marketing manager is experienced in maintaining computers and has done a wonderful job so far. But even she can't stop the march of progress."

"Your marketing manager?"

"Harriet Emerson. She'll be the liaison with your team. If anyone knows the ins and outs of the system, she does."

His stomach lurched and he swallowed. It would be too simple to find her on this first foray. Her name on the organisation's prospectus had brought him here. He hadn't expected it to be so easy. Or to affect his balance like this. He steadied his breathing, hoping his heart would follow.

"I look forward to working with her."

The man gaped and rushed into speech. "We didn't expect you here personally, Mr. Hall. Lucas. I'm sure Harriet will work well with whomever you designate."

On the other side of the room, Jimmie laughed and murmured something, and the blonde head bobbed up again.

A well-modulated voice, tinged with humour, carried easily as the woman responded to whatever was said. "So, where is this famous geek, Jimmie? I'm dying here, or at least the computer is."

Lucas stiffened, controlling the surge of adrenaline that threatened to derail his carefully cultivated facade. Smiling grimly, he looked down at the CEO.

"I'll certainly be involved, Gary. It's good to come down out of the ivory tower and see how an organisation like this is run." He raised his hand to stop the man from protesting further. "Please excuse me, I think I see someone I know."

Lucas strode across the room, drawn by the laughter.

He'd heard that voice, that familiar chuckle, before. The laughter stopped abruptly as Harriet Emerson looked up at him, mouth open as she sat at the desk, slender hands resting on the case of a dismantled desktop computer. Something flashed in her eyes, darkening them. *Shock?* She recovered quickly, her mouth stretching into a wide smile, showing even white teeth.

"Good grief, Jimmie, the geek is none other than Lucas Hall. What a blast from the past." She extended her arm, obviously expecting him to shake her hand. Jimmie watched the meeting wide-eyed so Lucas bit back the harsh words on the tip of his tongue. This was neither the time nor the place.

It irritated him when she remained seated, so he had to reach over the counter to take her hand. Still the princess, even after all this time.

She returned the grip confidently, her cool fingers wrapping around his. "Long time no see, Lucas. I'm sorry if I was rude. I've been fighting with these computers for days. I think they heard you were coming and decided to throw in the towel."

Withdrawing his hand, Lucas flexed it, disturbed by the contact and even more so by the casual greeting. As if she didn't remember how they'd parted. Of course, she had an image to maintain in front of her work colleagues. She was good at that. Maintaining an image.

All the same, it was hard to hold onto that long-ago memory with the reality of Harriet Emerson in front of him. He had to force himself to look beyond the beguiling face that had captured his unsuspecting heart seven years ago. To remember the rude awakening when he found she was just another rich girl out for a good time and none too pleased when things didn't go to plan.

Yet her smile now was almost too broad, too practiced. It didn't reach her eyes, which watched him warily.

With a mental shake of his head, Lucas moved back to his team, sending them to another job in the neighbouring suburb to fill in a couple of hours. He hadn't planned on staying beyond a quick reconnaissance, but Harriet Emerson had a lot of explaining to do. If that meant playing the technician for an hour or two, he was up for it.

He smiled at Jimmie who still hung over the counter, watching. An audience wasn't ideal, but he could work within those parameters. Pulling up another office chair, he moved it next to Harriet where she sat in front of the problem computer. She skittered away using the wheels of the chair and he compressed his lips. That pose of casual friendliness was just that, a pose. He'd very much like to see her away from the uncritical eyes of her work colleagues.

As his fingers moved among the components checking connections, she explained in a business-like manner what she'd done so far, her fair head close to his as she recited the long list of issues they'd had with this particular computer. He was aware of her oddly familiar, light floral scent. Her soft straight hair brushed against his shoulder and his groin tightened.

It had been a long time. *Too long.* And now it was too late. He wasn't here for that. Firming his jaw, he refocused on the computer, looking for potential weak spots.

It was all too familiar, bringing back other memories he'd thought forgotten but apparently were only suppressed. This computer was similar to one he used while doing his masters at university. Many an evening the younger Harriet had watched him tweaking and upgrading until she was just as familiar as he'd been with the insides of a computer.

With her intelligence and wealthy background, the last place he expected to find her was in an office job in a tiny charity. Hands resting on the case, he fixed her with a hard look. "I thought you planned on television journalism, Harriet. Travelling the world, working your way up to a position in current affairs."

She shrugged, stirring the long hair and sending another wave of her scent his way. "Plans change. You adapt to circumstance."

He moved uncomfortably, suddenly aware of shadowed cleavage as she bent forward. She was thinner than he remembered, but she'd always been finely boned. He'd liked that about her. How easy it had been to pick her up, carry her. He closed his eyes as memory flowed unbidden. Harriet, laughing as he carried her up the stairs of the old Queenslander and tossed her onto his bed. Pain tightened his chest and he beat it down with anger.

"You mean you didn't have what it takes, don't you? After all your big words when you dumped me."

Harriet blinked to hold back unexpected tears at his sudden attack. She'd known he'd be mad if they ever met again, knew she deserved his fury. But his surprise appearance hadn't allowed her time to adjust. To formulate a plan. She'd fallen back on her customary breezy veneer, but he'd poked and prodded at it with sharp eyes and blunt tongue, revealing its lack of substance.

Her instant recognition of Lucas Hall surprised her in one way. She remembered him as a rangy student in jeans and t-shirt, wearing a leather jacket. His night-dark hair was always too long and invariably messy from running his hands through it. This civilised stranger in the tailored suit with neatly cropped hair and elegant hands, clean of motorbike grease and oil, was a whole different ballgame.

But there was something in his eyes she couldn't help but recognise. The bright green was cooler, more reserved, but now and then a flicker of something caught at her memories.

She saw his throat work below the fashionable two-day old scruff on his strong jaw. He swallowed noticeably, his expression suggesting a bad taste in his mouth. Quickly, she turned to Jimmie, her voice husky as she struggled to hide her unruly emotions.

"Do you think you can run over to the café and pick up a coffee for Mr. Hall and a hot chocolate for me?"

She rummaged in a purse on the desk, handing over a large denomination note. "Do you still take your coffee black, Lucas?"

"Yes. No sugar."

Jimmie vanished in the direction of the lift and Lucas smirked "I'll give you marks for efficiency in disposing of the audience."

"I had no ulterior motive. He usually gets morning tea around now."

"He seems keen to do your bidding. You always had a knack for inspiring devotion?"

"Inspiring...? I don't know what you mean." Of all the things he could accuse her of, she'd not expected that one.

"Gary spent a lot of time singing your praises."

"You think I'm pretending to be some kind of plaster saint? You have to be kidding."

"Is it such a stretch?"

"Considering the money I've saved the organisation, I'm not surprised Gary raves. He's a bit like that. You probably noticed already. But that's all. He's married with a family. Which he raves about, given half a chance."

"Is there anyone?" His gaze dropped to her bare hands as he spoke. She looked down, aware the way she twisted them together gave away her inner turmoil. He'd always been able to read her body language. Back when they'd been together he'd been quick to comfort her, soothe her nervousness. Like before her school exams, and the ballet concert. He'd been so kind. This time he was armoured. Would use his knowledge against her.

She pulled her hands apart, rubbing them against her thighs. Why did it matter to him? "What's with the third degree, anyway? My personal life is none of your business."

He shrugged, the broad shoulders stretching the fine fabric of the shirt. "Just curious, I guess. They say you always remember your first." His lips curled in obvious distaste, as if that memory was sullied in some way. "So... Why marketing? In particular, why here? It's hardly prestigious and I don't imagine they pay as well as Corporate."

"Money isn't everything."

"True enough. What happened to your ambitions? If I recall correctly, you were going to be a household name as a journalist by twenty-five. You need to make better headway."

Rebellion at his constant niggling flared. "You were going to own your own company by twenty-five. How did that work out for you?"

His jaw tightened, and his mouth twisted slightly. "What makes you think I don't?"

She sighed, her hands fluttering in a movement of resignation. "You did it. This HeadWorks Group is your company." She looked away, unable to meet that hard stare. "I should have known."

"Why should you? It's been years. Anything could have happened."

"You had what it took, Lucas. At least one of us did."

A heaviness in his gut, Lucas watched her turn away to fiddle with some papers, leaning against the desk, defeat in the slump of her shoulders and the downturn of her mouth. He dragged his attention back to the task at hand, needing the distraction. He'd expected to feel triumphant, not this raw anger. He thought he'd gotten over that years ago. Like he thought...hoped...he'd got over wanting her.

He'd wanted her the first moment he saw her, all those years ago, a school senior at a university party she shouldn't have been at, staring at him with those dark blue eyes. Like he'd been hit with a laser fair square in the chest and his guts melted into a puddle at her feet. She'd asked him to dance and he'd looked at her weird, medieval type dress that reminded him of a character in the latest computer game and mumbled something about a Faerie Queen.

She'd eaten it up, her cheeks going all pink and splotchy. Back then, girls liked the look of him but ran when he opened his mouth. With her it didn't seem to matter. Whatever stupid words fell out of his mouth she accepted. She'd been willing to learn about his world of numbers, happy to hang with his geeky friends. He should have known it was too good to be true.

Taking the opportunity while she looked at the paperwork, he studied her, curious at the physical pull. He'd withdrawn back into his shell after what she'd done. Yet he couldn't help recalling what they'd had together. Mixed with her scent, the way her hair flowed over her shoulders, memories rushed back to clog his brain, rousing dormant emotions and reminding him of things he'd gone without for far too long.

A woman in his bed, for instance. He wasn't even going to count how long. His gaze lingered on the taut angle of her small breasts, pushed up as they rested on her outstretched arm on the desk in a characteristic pose, and his body stirred immediately.

He dismissed the memories impatiently as he turned back to the computer. He wasn't here to pick things up again. No matter that his body had other ideas. She was the past and this was about putting her there decisively. Tie up the loose ends from seven years ago. And after that...Closure.

Finding a broken cable connection on the motherboard, he used pliers to trim and re-attach the socket and after a quick test he put the computer back together again. Under Harriet's direction he slotted it back under the desk and plugged in the peripherals before booting it up, just as Jimmie returned with the hot drinks and a box of doughnuts.

Harriet's demeanour changed instantly, the smile back on her face as she took her drink and a pink iced doughnut.

"It's almost fixed, Jimmie, for the moment anyway."

If she was going for perky, it was overdone, but Jimmie didn't seem to see anything odd in her behaviour, handing Lucas his coffee and offering the doughnuts. Maybe this was how she usually behaved. The lad took his own coffee and the rest of the doughnuts and vanished down one of the hallways. She nodded briskly as she put her drink down.

"Nice."

Taking a deep breath, Harriet debated with herself how to keep the atmosphere cool and impersonal. If he started to ask questions, hung around to find out her secrets, she didn't know what would happen. It was already awkward. She'd snabbled the boss to do a basic computer repair. His strong features were reassuringly familiar but his eyes as they gleamed down at her were alien and unreadable.

"Shouldn't I be talking to one of your tech guys?"

"I'm quite competent, Harriet."

"It's not that. I know you are. But you own the company. This is hardly effective use of resources. At the very least." How stupid did she feel? She couldn't even talk to Lucas like a normal human being. A bit of a switch from when they first met.

He shrugged as he reached for his laptop. "I'm still quite capable of fixing redundant hardware. Besides, as it turns out, it gave me a chance to see what you're up to."

"It must have been a surprise." His brows rose, and she stumbled on. "Seeing me here."

"Not entirely. I saw your name on the application. It crossed my mind that it could be you."

*Crossed his mind? Like it wasn't important?* She stared at his averted face. *Or was it?*

"Did it bother you?" *What a stupid thing to say.* She ducked her head, pretending to study the screen as she hit a few random keys. Her heart was pounding in her chest. *He'd known she might be here and came anyway?* Had he wanted to see her? Why, after seven years did he suddenly have to roll back into her life? Her perfectly happy life. Well... contented...mostly.

"Why would it bother me? We're practically strangers these days."

"Of course. I just..." She let her words trail off. After

seven years she should have known better. Businesslike. That's what she needed to be, here and now. He mustn't see how his presence affected her. She quickly brought up the database. "I'd better get on with showing you the software. You must have more important things to do."

From the corner of her eye she saw him move closer and she swivelled on her chair to keep him from brushing against her legs. Preparing to launch into her spiel, she took an unwary breath, sucking in the taste of him, all citrus and faintly musk. Her stomach clenched, and she closed her eyes against another rush of tears.

This was way too reminiscent of the past. Sitting close while they worked on assignments. They'd both been so busy at the time, her with her senior year of school to finish, him doing his masters at university. The four years' age difference had worried her parents. But when they were alone together it didn't seem to matter.

There had been a comradeship even in studying together, side by side, thighs pressed together, arms brushing occasionally. She shot a quick glance his way, but he seemed indifferent, his eyes fixed on the screen, his beautifully sculpted mouth a straight line as he concentrated.

"Forward compatibility is getting to be a real problem." The words came out in a squeak and she cleared her throat and continued, losing her self-consciousness as she went on. This she knew back to front. Lucas leaned uncomfortably close as together they went through the various programs and databases used by the charity and discussed the different uses and outputs required for the day-to-day running of the organisation.

They were both totally involved in the task when Jimmie came to ask if they needed lunch.

Harriet looked up with a frown. "I'll just have a chicken wrap, thanks and a juice." She stopped to pick up her purse and handed Jimmie some cash before turning back to the problem at hand. Lucas pulled out his wallet and ordered the same but with coffee and a sweet muffin.

He frowned as he pushed his wallet into his back pocket. "You haven't changed much. I remember you always had a single-minded absorption in whatever task was at hand. Food be damned."

"And you were always hungry whatever time of day, day or night." She stared at him, hardly believing she'd come out with that. Personal was out. Shared memories were dangerous. She had to maintain a professional distance. His gaze caught hers, his mouth opened and then closed as he broke the contact. He'd obviously thought better of what he was about to say. Instead he turned back to his laptop, typing in that odd jerky pattern he'd used back when he was at university. So, he hadn't changed in some ways either.

While she rattled on about the specifics of the system they required to maintain the databases, the financials, tracking the government legislation and reporting, her mind was busy making notes about the tall figure beside her. His height certainly hadn't changed, he'd towered over her back then too, but his shoulders had filled out in the past seven years.

He'd been all lean muscle as a twenty-two-year-old, but his upper body hadn't fully developed despite his active lifestyle. Considering his chosen career Harriet would have expected him to stay lean but he must have done something to bulk up. It wasn't just the suit because he'd loosened his tie and taken off the jacket halfway through the morning and the white shirt in a fine silk weave did nothing to disguise the physique underneath.

The brilliant eyes were still as intense as ever, focusing on his laptop as he entered the information she was giving him at speed, flashing between different screens. The mouth though, there was something different there. She'd always loved the shape, the full lower lip and the perfect bow of the thinner upper one. How many times had she traced those lips with the tip of her finger, run her nail along the crescent shape of the dimple on the left-hand side?

Drawing in a sharp breath, she stole a look at Lucas as he frowned over the laptop. The corners of his mouth tucked in, drawing long lines down each side, but there was no sign of the dimple. Even when he'd smiled up at Jimmie, the creases stayed, ageing him beyond his twenty-nine years.

The return of his team brought her back to reality. The group stood waiting by the door for Lucas to join them, a man and two women in more casual clothes than the corporate suit their employer chose to wear. She watched them talk amongst themselves, wondering what he was saying, and they scattered, wielding tablet computers and a tape measure.

When he joined her again, standing beside the desk, she ventured a comment. "It really brings it home when I see your minions doing your bidding."

"We're a team. I don't believe in top down management."

"I only meant about you having your own company. Employing heaps of people."

"Not a big number. Less than one hundred in the parent company. Quite a few in the subsidiaries and overseas. I'm not sure about exact numbers. It changes all the time, depending on projects and contracts. Cyber security is still our core business, following on from my research project for the doctorate. It's too specialised for any but the big corporates and governments. We do a lot with the military, here and overseas."

She'd known that was where he was headed but it made it so much more incomprehensible that he should come here. "That sounds remarkable. Consider me impressed." She smiled, hoping for a response but he simply nodded.

"It was hard work. Time consuming. But I had nothing else to distract me." Harriet wondered if that was a reference to their last meeting, but his eyes moved away to look at his notes and she realised the conversation was over. She'd called him a distraction she couldn't afford. But the other things she'd said had been worse.

Suddenly, she was anxious for him to be gone. At least Jimmie was back, a bag with the lunch order dangling from one hand, coffee in the other. "You're a busy man. If you go with Jimmie, he'll show you where the server and network switch are plugged in. I'll follow in a minute. I just need to wrap up here."

"I'm in no hurry. I'll wait for you."

He obviously had no intention of leaving the reception area without her. At least it was just him and Jimmie. His team had vanished into the back rooms of the building. She reached for her gloves.

Lucas watched her pull on what looked like leather golfing gloves that left her fingers free, wriggling the bare, slender digits as she closed the Velcro at her wrist.

She spoke briskly. "You can get on with your lunch, Jimmie. We'll be along shortly. I'll show Mr. Hall where the heart of the monster resides first."

Bracing her hands on the counter, Harriet pushed

herself up into a standing position. She seemed to stumble, a gasping breath escaping her lips. Automatically he stepped forward to help, freezing at an urgent shake of the head from Jimmie. Moving back, out of the way, he schooled his expression and received a thumbs-up from the lad.

Fiddling with the stack of brochures on the counter, he watched silently as Harriet used the bench-top to steady herself. Half expecting her to straighten up and walk away, her shuffling gait as she moved sideways along the desk sent a shiver of unease down his spine.

His gaze dropped to her legs, stiff and awkward in the loose cut slacks that matched the neat, pale blue blouse. Reaching the end of the desk, she flopped down in the wheelchair he'd noticed earlier. Not what he expected. Stomach churning, he took a deep breath to settle it and followed her down the hallway.

2

_____

*H*arriet waited for him with her wheelchair positioned in front of her desk, the server and switch in the special cabinet beside it. She'd expected more of a reaction when she'd been forced to walk. That he would say something. In that first moment he appeared surprised, even shocked. He'd looked away immediately, but she'd seen nausea in the compressed lips and the way he swallowed.

Of course, he would be repulsed by her ungainly movements. He'd always said... She closed her eyes. He'd said so many things, in his abrupt awkward way about how he'd loved the way she moved, how he loved to watch her dance.

Getting up in front of Lucas felt far worse than displaying her clumsiness in front of colleagues who'd never met her prior to the accident. Unlike most of the people she knew these days, he would remember the Harriet from before the accident. Not this hollow somebody, going through the motions.

Footsteps sounded on the vinyl floor of the hallway and

she clenched her hands tightly to stop the trembling. She was stronger than this. Stronger than the girl she'd been seven years ago.

He paused in the doorway and she saw him taking in the setup with the desk cut-out and lowered keyboard drawer.

"Gary had my workstation altered for me, but the rest are at the wrong height, as you saw up front. I can't get my chair close enough."

"We need to meet. After work."

His sudden demand startled her into meeting his eyes. Ice green, they held an imperative it was hard to resist. "I'm busy."

"Don't you think you owe me an explanation?"

She knew it was coming, but it didn't make it any easier knowing he was right. "What do you want to know?"

"You told me after the accident you would only be in plaster for a few weeks and then it would be back to normal."

"I was over-optimistic, it would appear."

"Come off it, Harry, you lied to me and I want to know why."

*Why?* That was something she could never explain. Not to the young passionate Lucas, and certainly not to this distant, cool stranger. "Look, I was eighteen. You remember how invincible you feel when you're young. That nothing bad could possibly happen. Maybe I didn't want to face reality."

"And what was reality? Was there a spinal injury after all?"

"No, I didn't lie about that. It was only my knees. They... didn't mend as well as I expected...hoped." She fixed him with an unwavering stare, willing him to leave it at that.

He returned her gaze, green eyes glinting. Suddenly he

turned away, rolling his shoulders as if to relieve tension. "Fair enough. We'll leave it, for the moment. This isn't the time. Show me the server and then I'll grab my lunch and talk through things with my guys." He turned back as she let her breath go. "This isn't finished, Harriet Emerson. We will talk."

After he'd gone, Harriet folded her arms around her midriff and closed her eyes. Why now, when she had made some kind of life without him? He'd said, you never forget your first. She'd never had a chance to add a second and third or more, as he must have over the years. What man would take on a woman in a wheelchair? Would want to make love to a woman he needed to treat like china in case she broke?

Jimmie's voice broke into her thoughts. "Harriet? Are you okay?"

She looked up into his worried face, bringing up her usual smile with an effort. "I'm fine, I just realised I forgot to have my lunch. Have the HeadWorks people gone?"

"Your friend went away but the others are still around. I heard him tell them he'll be back later."

It was almost time to go home when a tingling awareness alerted her to his return. He came to sit beside her again, disturbingly virile. She'd had to abandon her office when his technical people came to inspect the server but now she was back, trying to get the most urgent jobs done before they laid waste to the system. She had hoped to get the newsletter done at least, but the mail-merge had crashed the system. They seemed quite confident the whole computer network would be replaced but it would come down to Lucas.

He lay the plan of the office she given him on the desk and opened his laptop. "I have to see Gary for final confirmation so we can go ahead but thought I would get your opinion on what I've drawn up." He sat far too close and because of the constraints of her chair, Harriet couldn't move away without being obvious. Her throat tightened at the thought that after all they'd been to each other, it came down to this...this distance between them despite the physical proximity.

Focusing on the plans rather than the hint of clean soap emanating from his warm flesh, she listened carefully as Lucas outlined a new system that included options for high speed broadband and Wi-Fi throughout the office. "That all sounds great, but it also sounds expensive. Can't we just upgrade what we've got?"

"You've already upgraded everything to within an inch of its life. The only way to go is to get rid of everything and begin again."

Frowning, Harriet stared blankly at the computer screen where the error message was still blinking ominously. "How much will it be all up? On my estimation, I don't think our budget will cover even the half of it."

"And that's where my company will come in. We'll do the whole thing at no cost to you apart from the inconvenience while we set it up. New everything with as much future proofing as we can build in."

It was hard to take in. "Do you have the authority to make that sort of commitment, Lucas?"

"It's my company. I answer to a board, but I have discretion with the Community Technology Assistance Fund."

He left the room abruptly and Harriet sucked in a breath. It was overwhelming. Unbelievable. Her mind spun at the implications. *All of it.* It would be worth tens of thousands of dollars. If anything, that brought home the difference between the Lucas from the past and this corporate high flyer.

She assumed he'd gone after his meeting with the CEO, so she was surprised when he turned up at the door of her office just before closing time. "It's all sorted. We'll start tomorrow. Is there anything urgent that needs to be done within the next week?"

Harriet sighed, looking at her screen. "Just the newsletter. It keeps collapsing when I do the mail merge."

"Hang on, I'll be right back." He vanished from the doorway but reappeared again with his laptop and planted himself beside her. She tried not to squirm away when his arm brushed hers, raising goose-bumps that prickled under the skin of her arms and upper body. It was odd. He used to hate being physically close to people. She'd been one of the few exceptions but that was a long time ago.

"Show me what needs doing."

He dived into the task, moving files and setting them up on the laptop, swapping cables to the printer and within twenty minutes the newsletters were finally printing. Harriet moved away, spinning one wheel with accustomed ease to bring her close enough to check the finished product, glad to breathe air that smelled of ink and machinery instead of...Lucas.

"This is brilliant. We can email the bulk of them, but we have someone coming in tomorrow to get a percentage ready for postage and I thought we might have to cancel. I appreciate the help. I suspect computer repairs and printing glitches are a bit below your pay grade."

He smiled tightly at that. "It's good to keep my hand in."

"I suppose you have to do a lot more talking than playing with computers these days."

"Selling the product means I have to do presentations,

but I still spend most of my time in research and development. I have a reliable management team I can leave with the routine stuff."

"I'm guessing you don't have a problem presenting in public these days."

He stiffened as he unplugged the last of the cables. *Why had she invoked that particular memory?* Guilt soured the back of her throat as Lucas turned slowly, meeting her eyes, his own bleak and cold.

"No. Not at all."

Almost tangible between them, the recollection of his bumbling efforts to express any thought other than the technical language he felt comfortable in when they first met. The long hours leading up to his face to face interview for the prestigious research place at UCLA when she'd coached him using techniques learned in her drama classes, ensuring he was word perfect.

His mouth tightened and then curled up slightly in a sneer. He'd be remembering how she used it against him at their last meeting. His shoulders twitched in a half shrug.

"I guess you were right, practice does makes perfect."

He started to pack up and Harriet closed her computer and grabbed her bag ready to head home, tucking it onto her lap. It was just as well the newsletter was under control as Thursday was one night when she had to get away on time.

As she wheeled down the corridor, Lucas joined her, still looking grim. To break the uncomfortable silence, she asked about what was to happen tomorrow.

"I suppose we won't see you again. You have your minions to do all the hard yards I imagine."

Halting at the lift, Lucas hesitated, unsure of what to say. He didn't usually do more than a token visit, but this was different. Her pointed reminder of his youthful inadequacies had struck a sore spot. Maybe she hadn't meant it that way, but it reminded him of how he'd felt when she'd turned on him so unexpectedly in the hospital.

It didn't seem to matter that he'd got over them. That he had no problem dealing with business communication, though personal interactions still made him nervous. He rubbed the back of his neck, easing the tension. It was difficult to get used to looking so far down when talking to her.

"I'll have several teams doing the work, but I'll come by before it's finished. I like to see projects through." *And I'd like the chance to ask a few more questions.* "I'll no doubt see you at some point."

Exiting the lift in the car park, Harriet went immediately to a red hatchback sitting in the disabled parking bay right beside the lifts. He hesitated as they parted, wondering if she needed assistance but she waved at him dismissively with a muttered goodbye. From his BMW, in a nearby position, he had a perfect view of the Ford Focus with the metal hoist on the roof. He watched her open the driver's door and manoeuvre her wheelchair close to the seat.

She used her hands to lever herself into the car and pull her legs in after her. Activating the hoist, she closed the wheelchair and hooked it on, waiting while it was pulled onto the roof of the car above her seat. When she closed the door, he started his car and drove away, his gut churning again. After all these years of nursing his resentment, it was surprising to find it being challenged as he saw more of the woman who'd changed his life for both better and worse.

"It's no good, is it?"

Dragging his attention back to his companion, Lucas smiled ruefully. "Sorry, Angela. My mind isn't on the job."

"You aren't even doing the meal justice. At a thousand dollars a head, you could at least try and get your money's worth by eating the steak."

Picking up his cutlery, he hesitated. He considered Angela a friend, but only in relation to the work place. He kept his private life separate. "Why did you invite me? You know I'm not into the social round. I usually just send money to these charity events."

"I know. You'd much rather be at home playing with your software, and I mean that in the strictest sense of the term. I wanted your company of course." She laughed throatily. "I seem to be full of double-entendre's tonight."

Alerted by something in her voice, he looked up. Her honey blonde hair was piled on her head in a sophisticated style that looked unbelievably complicated, her immaculately made up face, model perfect. No one would guess the five-year age advantage she had on him. Her mouth, red and lush had a humorous quirk that wasn't reflected in her sherry coloured eyes.

They were giving out signals that set off alarm bells. He looked away, staring down at his hand, at the pale band of skin on his ring finger. The mark was fading rapidly but he still wasn't ready. And he still had to deal with present day Harriet Emerson. "Ange..."

"Don't say it, Lucas. I already get the message."

"You're a beautiful woman."

"But it's not enough, is it?"

"Not for me. Not right now. But...I'm the classic

computer nerd. Happier playing with my software...in the strictest sense of the term."

She laughed and the expression in her eyes softened. "You're probably right. We work too well together to put it at risk for something that isn't going anywhere. Besides, I've already won the pool. Enough to buy myself a nice pair of Jimmy Choo's."

"What pool."

"The one running here in your head office. Betting on who would manage to break through and get you to go on a date."

He didn't know whether to be offended or flattered. The idea that people were watching him, commenting on his lack of social life was faintly disturbing. Maybe they had too much leisure time. He might have to do something about that. "You made enough to buy designer shoes? That's some serious money."

"It's been running for over a year. Ever since you came back more or less permanently from the U.S."

"I see. And you claimed the pool on the grounds of me agreeing to partner you to this dinner."

She licked her lips nervously and took a long swig of champagne. Maybe she'd remembered his reputation for not having a sense of humour. "Within the terms of the bet this counted. Is it a problem?"

"There speaks the lawyer. No, it isn't a problem. But I'd be grateful if you would discourage any further such...outbreaks."

"Absolutely. In any case the drought is broken so they'll probably lose interest."

"I hope so." Her face remained slightly flushed. He was too socially inept to be a suitable long-term escort for someone like Angela. Not when she was used to class acts.

Like her world-famous journalist ex. "Have you heard anything from Stef since he left?"

The colour in her face deepened. "No. Last I heard he was in Eastern Europe. I'm sorry Lucas. I shouldn't have mentioned the betting pool."

"Changing the subject? Very well. Perhaps you can answer a question for me. On the strength of those Jimmy Choo's."

Warily she nodded, her fingers gripping the stem of her glass. "Of course."

"Why do women lie?"

"What a strange question." Her body language changed instantly, from defensive to alert. "Do you mean habitual lying? As in criminal behaviour. Or normal women who would usually be honest."

"The latter."

Placing her champagne glass on the table she cocked her head, scrutinising him intently. "I suppose you won't tell me the story." She snickered. "I take it that look means no? Very well. Sometimes we might lie out of pride or hurt feelings. Maybe to save someone else's feelings. I think most women I know would lie to save someone they love from being hurt. We're emotional creatures at heart."

Lucas nodded, shifting his gaze to the half-eaten meal. "That's pretty much what I thought."

"Does it help?"

"Maybe. I just have to figure out which one of the above."

"Is it important?" Her hand came to rest on his and the flash of a camera jolted him from the reverie. He withdrew his hand smoothly as the photographer moved onto the next table.

"Probably not. But I like everything clear cut. I don't like loose ends."

Picking up the champagne she grinned, "Tell me something I didn't know."

He forced himself to laugh. "I'm that easy to read."

"No." Angela shook her head. "No, you're not."

"What's that supposed to mean?"

"You're a complete enigma to most of your staff. There was even a suggestion that a man might win the dating pool bet."

"You can reassure yourself on that one. But I don't see that my employees need to concern themselves with my personal life."

Her finger lightly brushed the faded mark on his hand. "They can't help wondering. Widowed or divorced?"

"Stupidity. One of those dim-witted things you do when you think with other parts of your anatomy instead of your brain."

"What happens in Vegas?"

He looked away, focusing on the swirling dancers. It was as good a diversion as any. "Something like that. Five minutes in that crazy town and anyone could get sucked in."

"It's over?"

"It never really began. But that doesn't make my life open slather."

"You're a phenomenon, Lucas. A software billionaire with an international presence. With just a touch of mystery. Its natural people are interested. It doesn't hurt that you aren't a skinny weed with coke-bottle glasses."

No, his looks had never been the issue. "Can we get off this subject? I don't think my skull will cope with the undue expansion of my ego."

Laughing, she agreed, leading the conversation into innocuous waters.

Sometime later, as they circled the dance floor, he was jolted out of his comfort zone again by the mention of a name. "Who did you say it was?"

"John Favreau from Emerson, Schwartz and Cooper."

"Is that Jack Emerson's firm?"

"Yes. Do you know him?"

"I met him years ago. Have you come across him? He's in your field, isn't he?"

"More than in my field. When I was studying, he was the man to be. Top corporate lawyer in the state and probably among the top in the country. Government had him on tap as an advisor. I understand he still does some advisory work since he semi-retired."

"I didn't realise he'd cut back on work."

"Is it a problem? Were you wanting to consult with him?" She sounded slightly affronted.

"Of course not. We're perfectly happy with your work. I was just surprised. He wasn't that old."

"True enough. It was for family reasons. His daughter was smashed up in an accident. An only child. I understand it was pretty rough on the family. Especially as it had happened before."

Lucas missed a step and apologised tersely. "Before?"

"They lost a son. Years ago, now. Before I graduated."

Something Harriet hadn't talked about. "Sounds like the daughter's accident was common knowledge."

"Not at all. I was working with John Favreau on a class action at the time. I had the insider goss."

He knew the answer, but something forced the words out. "What sort of accident?"

"She was out with her boyfriend on a motorbike when a

truck ran into them. Poor kid. The boyfriend received only minor injuries. It was her graduation night too. That seems to happen way too often."

Struggling for something to say that wouldn't give away his inner turmoil he eventually found a suitable but inadequate response. "Yes. I believe so."

It was a relief to deliver his date home at the end of the night. He needed time to think.

She extended her hand with a wry smile. "Thanks, Lucas. If I ask you out again would you accept?"

"I haven't been great company. I'm sure you can do better."

"I'm not asking for more than a date for the odd function. Since Stef left, it's...awkward. People are used to us being a couple and now they don't know what to say. I've some more charity functions between now and the end of the year that I must attend, and they expect me to be a plus one. If Stef were still here it would be different."

Hunching his shoulders, Lucas considered her request. She was a damn good lawyer and good to work with. He owed her for all the help she'd given making the transition from the US. "I'll help you out for the odd thing, but only as a last resort."

Her teeth gleamed in the light from her door. "You won't regret it. I'll even pay for the tickets."

"I'll pay for my own. But thank you anyway."

Driving home, he wondered if he'd done the right thing. Not the sex thing. Two lonely people thinking of someone else was nothing but trouble in the long run. Trouble he didn't need. She'd been right about them working well together. He'd been out of touch after the years in L.A. and her knowledge of Australian corporate law was extensive.

But if people were already talking about him... Tossing the car keys on the kitchen bench, he poured himself a glass of water. What did it matter anyway? He was near enough to single, even if he didn't feel it...

The light on his landline was flashing and he groaned inwardly. Why his mother couldn't just ring his mobile and be done with it? He listened to the rambling message twice before deleting it. It was nice to know she didn't keep her criticisms for her youngest son. He'd have to go to the aged care home tomorrow and sort it out. Which meant he wouldn't have time to drop in to LearnAble and speak to Harriet.

Oh, yes, Harriet Emerson. The one thing his snob of a mother thought he did right. She wouldn't believe the break hadn't been his fault, his choice. *You're just like your father. All looks and no substance. You can't even talk like a normal human being.* It still amazed him that classy Rosemary Telford had married his taciturn tradesman father.

His sister Jocelyn, in her usual forthright manner, said she'd fallen in lust with him and it was true that the eldest, Paul, had been substantially premature even for a "Honeymoon baby". Her resentment had coloured all their lives. His siblings had left home at the first opportunity. With less options, Ted Hall had simply keeled over and died on the job.

Checking his schedule, he slotted in a visit to the well-appointed residential facility. It would have been so easy to do what had to be done from the safety and distance of his Malibu home. The long incoherent letters had been easier to handle than face to face interactions. But with Paul tied up in England with his wife's family business and Jocelyn in

Canada with her husband, he was the logical choice to come home and keep an eye on their ailing mother.

His business could be run from anywhere and the state government had offered good incentives to bring the lucrative company back to Australia. The temptation to look up old friends had come later.

Harriet arrived home from her basketball game tired and sore. It had kept her mind off Lucas but only until she parted from her team mates. Memories long held back were hammering at her brain. *How could a few months so many years ago, matter so much?* Sitting in the shower, she sponged herself down under the pounding water. Forcing back the memories was as futile as holding back the tides.

Tucking herself into bed, Harriet dragged a pillow under her legs and set her laptop on her knees. She only really used it for work, keeping her social media presence around the organisation. It was too much of a time suck otherwise, and her friendships were mostly local. Picking up the memory stick from the bedside table she hesitated, guilt nudging at her. Years ago, her mother had taken everything else away. Everything that remained of her time with Lucas. She hadn't known about the photos and Harriet didn't remind her.

It had seemed harsh at the time. Looking back from this distance, remembering how worried her parents had been about her, Harriet understood why. The agreement she'd made with them kept the USB stick untouched in the bottom of her jewellery box. The one with the dancing ballerina her parents gave her when she'd passed her first RAD exam.

Now Lucas was back in her life, albeit temporarily, so surely there could be no harm in glancing through old photographs. Compressing her lips, she put the stick into the port on the laptop, jumping nervously as the computer signalled its readiness. As the first picture flashed onto the screen, she sucked in a deep breath. She'd almost forgotten that photo.

Taken by the school friend who'd persuaded her into attending the party put on by her university aged sister, it was a little fuzzy. But the memories it represented rose sharp and clear as crystal. She still had the long flowing purple dress and the jewelled hair clips but she never wore them.

Releasing her breath with a sigh, she let her mind go back to that first time. To the place she never let herself go. The first time she'd seen Lucas Hall.

*The growl of the black Ducati motorbike drowned out the heavy throb of the music behind her as she sat on the steps of the old timber house, watching the late arrival. In leathers, a matt black helmet in one hand, he was every good girl's wet dream. His emerald eyes glowed as he looked at her and he smiled. She was lost from that moment, the dimple in his cheek, the intensity of those amazing eyes stealing her previously untouched heart.*

*She called him James Dean and he laughed and called her a Faery Queen muttering something about a computer game. They danced briefly, silently, and afterwards he kept her close as he hung with his mates, hardly talking.*

It was heaven until he discovered her age, returning her home on the back of his bike and parting with a regretful brush of his lips over hers and a firm goodbye.

Flicking through the images on the screen, she smiled ruefully. It hadn't been goodbye but perhaps it would have been better for both of them if he'd remained firm. The flush of popularity that exploded in the Senior Common Room following his appearance in full black leather glory outside the school several weeks later had gone to her head just a little. Miss Goody-Two-Shoes dating the biker dude from the wrong side of town was more than a nine-day wonder at her exclusive all girl's school. She'd foolishly thought it would last forever.

Brushing tears away, Harriet returned to the present reluctantly, still caught in the magic of the might have been. Those few months following that first meeting had defined her life. As if it was only then she'd been fully alive. Awakened from slumber by the light in a pair of vivid green eyes, like the Fae creature he'd named her. Called from another realm only to be lost in a world suddenly empty.

She rubbed her stomach, pushing away the ache. Dreams were empty things that left you wanting. Long ago she'd decided to have no more truck with dreams. But now Lucas was back and they crept into her soul like dark shadows, reminding her of all she couldn't have.

**3**

———

*I*t was all finished and he hadn't come. She should be glad of it but somehow the ache in her chest seemed to get bigger each day that went by without him. Considering the previous twenty-five hundred or so days when she hadn't seen him, the reaction seemed excessive. But her heart had been aching all the time, under the anaesthetising grief of her loss. That was why smiling came so hard, why she had to pretend.

His people were amazing, coming in teams and targeting each aspect of the transition with unparalleled efficiency. The disruption to operations had been minimal, even with the refit of the reception desk to make it wheelchair friendly. The cabinet makers hadn't stopped there, completely refurbishing the shelving in the waiting area and building in cupboards to store a lot of the equipment. Now the last of the workmen and technicians had gone.

Taking refuge in her office, she tried to get excited over the speed and sparkly newness of everything. It had taken a couple of days to get used to the latest versions of the software but now everything was running smoothly. With a final few keystrokes she sent the latest reports to the fancy new printer. At this rate, she'd be almost out of a job. Looking after the ageing computer system had taken more hours than she'd realised.

"Harriet?"

Startled she twisted her head around to identify the strangely familiar voice. "Graeme? Graeme Mac Alistair?" He'd shared the old Queenslander with Lucas and a couple of other computer science students while they were at university. The brawny, ginger haired giant nodded. "I couldn't believe it when Lucas told me you worked here." He advanced with his arms outstretched, his large hands swooping down to frame her face. The kiss was a loud smack accompanied by a gentle stroke of one hand down her hair.

"Let me look at you, girl." His pale blue eyes flicked up and down. "I do believe you're shorter than you used to be."

With a rueful laugh, she nodded. "That's truer than you know. What brings you here?"

"Just dropping off a few things for your set up. Some laptops and tablets for your outreach staff. I could have let Lucas have all the fun but after all this time, I wanted to see you."

"You work with Lucas?"

"I run the hardware side of things." He planted himself on the edge of her desk and folded his arms over the broad chest. "So, what on earth have you done to yourself?"

"Crocked my knees in that accident. Didn't Lucas tell you?"

"The man is still like a clam when it comes to nattering about his personal life."

"I don't think I count as personal life. Not anymore."

"I suppose not. Couldn't believe it when he said you'd

broken it off back in the day." He looked down at the wheelchair. "I suppose under the circs it was just as well. You couldn't have gone to the U.S. with him like that. How bad is it?"

"Pretty much all the bones from here to here were crushed when the bike landed on me." Her hands framed the distance from mid-thigh to mid-calf.

"You can't walk?"

"I can use crutches for short distances. One leg can weight bear for short periods. They bolted me back together as well as they could, but the soft tissue damage means the joints are weak and floppy."

"Is it painful?"

"Only a bit when I walk. Otherwise I'm fine. I wear braces to support the joints."

"And Lucas walked away? Left you to go through all that alone?"

Harriet flinched under the brutality of his words and he nodded. "He didn't know how bad it was, did he?"

"No."

"You didn't want him getting all noble, I suppose. The pair of you were as crazy as each other. He would have stayed if he'd known."

"That couldn't happen, Grae. It was a chance in a lifetime."

"Yeah. Some guys get all the luck and still miss out on the important things."

He stood and cracked his knuckles. "Lucas is around somewhere, finalizing the ongoing maintenance contract with your boss. I better go find him." He punched her lightly on the shoulder. "Don't be a stranger, Harry. Keep in touch."

She watched him turn away, her heart beating overtime

at the information that Lucas was in the building. When he let out a crude exclamation, she jerked around in her chair.

Graeme thumped the intruder on the shoulder and Harriet flinched in sympathy. "For chrissakes, Lucas, don't sneak up on a guy like that." He darted a quick glance back at her and she guessed he was having the same thought. How long had Lucas been standing at the door and what had he heard?

Looking at their guilty expressions, Lucas wanted to laugh. But the anger surging below the surface wouldn't let him. Not just from seeing the easy camaraderie of the pair of them, but at the revealing nature of the conversation. He could have believed her sincere in her supposed sacrifice if he didn't know better. It seemed Graeme was willing to believe her. It certainly made sense and fitted with everything he'd thought he'd known about Harriet Emerson.

But it didn't explain everything. It didn't explain the things she'd said when she hadn't known he was there, outside the hospital room. She'd said right from the start she didn't blame him for the accident. Was that a lie too? Truth, lies...he didn't know what to believe any more. He nodded to Graeme. "We're expected in the staff room. Some kind of afternoon tea ceremony."

"Good. I'm starving." Graeme plunged out the door and could be heard whistling as he vanished in the direction of the staff room.

Harriet frowned after him. "How does he know where to go?"

"He'll have the map of the place in his head. He put

together the system for you using the information we gave him."

"How long as he worked for you?"

"Since I moved the company here, so about thirteen months."

He could see her mulling over that, wondering perhaps why he'd come back, why he hadn't come looking before. He'd been looking all right. Just not in the right places. Maybe he'd been reluctant to find her. Afraid that she would still wield that strange power over his heart. He hadn't known the extent of her lies back then.

"I suppose we better get to the staff room if Gary is waiting."

Stepping in front of her, he forced her to stop moving, her hands resting lightly on the push rims of the wheels. "Have you been in touch with Graeme while I've been overseas? With any of the old group?"

"No, I lost touch. I haven't seen Graeme since he visited me in hospital just before..."

He knew what brought her to a halt. His own disastrous visit. "I was surprised at how...friendly...you were. I only rated a handshake."

She snorted, angling her head to look up at him. "I doubt if you even wanted that much from me."

"You make the mistake of assuming too much about me. Like you did after the accident. Was that true? What you said to Graeme."

"Probably. Not that you were supposed to hear."

"You thought I couldn't cope."

"That didn't come into it. You were going overseas. I couldn't come. It was pointless prolonging the situation."

"You don't think I deserved the opportunity to discuss options?"

"There were no options."

"You're so stubborn. That hasn't changed."

Harriet couldn't help laughing. "Pot...kettle..."

His face softened. The old argument rose fresh between them. His chuckle was balm for her soul. How she missed their interactions. He might not have talked much in the old days, but they'd laughed all the time.

Something electric arced as their eyes locked. A quiver like the touch of ghostly fingers trickled down her spine as his pupils darkened, expanded. He leaned into her, resting his hands on the low metal side rails of her chair. It brought his face to her level, his exhalation lightly caressing her cheek. "What else hasn't changed, Harry?"

She could taste coffee on his breath, triggering her salivary glands but her lips felt dry and tight. Closing her eyes to block out his closeness, she dipped her tongue out to moisten her lips. Her body thrummed with sensation, coming alive again to his proximity. This couldn't happen. "I'm not..."

The words were swallowed as his mouth assaulted hers, hard and forceful, pushing her back, the wheelchair rocking under the impact. She tightened her grip on the wheel rims, but he'd done the same, pulling her closer. Her lips were pressed against her teeth, almost painful, the rebound of the chair forcing the clash. An ache began in her throat and she scrunched her lids tighter. She. Must. Not. Cry.

It was heaven. It was hell. It was over, the chair rocking back as he released her. He spun away, his hand going to his face, pinching the bridge of his nose. Surely it hadn't affected him that way as well? Almost immediately he faced her again, bright emerald eyes the only outward sign of his disturbance. If anything, the creases beside his mouth were deeper, pulling the corners down grimly.

"I'm sorry. I guess I'm out of practice."

"You kiss women in wheelchairs often?"

Colour mantled his cheekbones. "It's a first for me." He handed her a crisp white handkerchief, pulled from his pocket.

Looking up from the neatly folded linen she shook her head. "I don't need this. I'm not that upset."

His hand wavered towards her and then pointed to his bottom lip. "You might want to clean up."

Dabbing the handkerchief to her mouth, she examined it curiously, surprised to see a small drop of blood smeared over the fabric. "Oh." She dabbed again and another drop appeared, bright against the pristine white. "I didn't realise."

Lucas thrust his hands into his pockets, pushing back the jacket, displaying his narrow hips and waist. "Sorry. I didn't mean that to happen."

Something stirred in the pit of her stomach and she wanted to cry again for all they'd been together. Giving the soiled hanky more attention than it needed, she kept her face lowered. "I'll wash it and get it back to you."

"I buy them by the dozen, so you might as well chuck it."

Surprise bought her chin up. "Your mother doesn't buy them for you now?"

"She's in a nursing home. She had a fall over a year ago."

That explained much. "You came back for her."

That sounded a bit needy. Like there was any hope of him even thinking about an ex who'd dumped him in the most humiliating way possible. Twelve months of nothing pretty much proved he had no interest in looking her up. Despite the kiss. Pressing her lips together, she could feel them, slightly swollen and tender from his kiss. *Why on earth had he kissed her?*

*Why on earth had he kissed her?* Lucas didn't consider himself delusional but analysing that question was all kinds of wrong. It was very simple, in fact. He wanted to. Had done from the first time she'd popped her head over the reception desk. But he knew it was the wrong thing to do. She was beyond his reach.

Even more so now. She'd made it clear he wasn't good enough all those years ago, and now... Now she thought he wouldn't have the balls to take on a woman in a wheelchair. Watching her speed down the hallway ahead of him, he wondered if she was right.

Churned up as he was, Lucas didn't look forward to the small celebration. Fortunately, Gary spoke enough for all of them and with a few nods and smiles, a mouthful of scone and verbal support from Graeme, he made it through.

Most of the staff had trickled away when Jimmie sidled up to him holding a newspaper. "I saw your picture."

"Really?" Usually his P.A. kept him informed of any media interest. When he saw the photograph, he understood why. Darren wouldn't have been checking the weekend social pages. He was so rarely in them. Angela looked good and he looked...interested. They were holding hands, appearing totally immersed in each other. And they say a picture can't lie.

He glanced across at Harriet, deep in discussion with Graeme. *Had she seen it?* She looked up at that moment, her eyes on Jimmie. That strained smile that so irritated him hovered and then faded as she turned back to her conversation.

Harriet was conscious of Lucas staring at her and she wondered if she had donut icing on her face. Cautiously she ran her tongue over her still tender lips and his lashes flickered down and up. Graeme beckoned to him and he came over, closely followed by Jimmie.

Graeme spoke directly to Lucas. "I have to go, mate. I've a meeting in half an hour at head office." With a brisk hand shake for the awestruck Jimmie and friendly pat on Harriet's head she couldn't object to, he was gone, leaving the three of them alone.

Jimmie was absorbed in his newspaper, sounding out the caption silently when Lucas dropped into a crouch beside her chair. He looked slightly dishevelled as if he'd been running his long fingers through his short hair. "I was wondering if you'd like to come to dinner tonight. To celebrate the end of the project." He kept his voice low and Harriet wondered if she heard him right. He saw her confusion and smiled wryly. "We should talk."

Harriet was thinking furiously. And it wasn't just about her existing commitments for the evening. The photo of Lucas Jimmie was carting around everywhere, showed him with a gorgeous leggy blonde with the all the usual obvious advantages, plus the one that she could probably stand on her own two feet. Harriet was so not going there. "I don't think so, Lucas. We're going to a basketball game, aren't we?" Jimmie looked startled but nodded.

Lucas looked a little startled as well. "Okay, some other time perhaps."

From his tone he probably thought it was just an excuse and all things considered she probably would have made one if she didn't have a genuine commitment, so she could hardly blame him.

She was just starting to relax, having jumped that hurdle with a modicum of success, when Jimmie in his wisdom almost gave her a heart attack. "You could come with us, Lucas. Come to the basketball tonight."

Forcing a laugh Harriet shook her head, "I'm sure Lucas has better things to do than go to an amateur basketball match." With a shrewd glance at both of them Lucas nodded to Jimmie. "I'd like to come, thanks. What time and how do we get there?"

Stifling a sigh as she saw the pleased expression on the face of her work colleague Harriet brought up a perky smile. "Seven p.m. start. At the auditorium at St. Pat's. I think you know where that is."

Lucas looked at her face rather grimly and nodded. "Does anyone need a lift?"

Promptly at a quarter to seven Lucas was sitting with Jimmie in the third row, half way along the near empty auditorium. Looking at the steps Lucas had been doubtful, but Jimmie insisted they always sat in that spot without fail.

Taking a bag of peanuts from the selection he'd picked up from a vending machine, Lucas looked at his watch, worried that he couldn't see Harriet. It was only five minutes to go and he was starting to think she'd stood them up when Jimmie nudged him and pointed to the door where a group of basketball players had gathered. "She's number five."

Wheel chair basketball. Lucas was fast thinking he

shouldn't have been surprised. This last week had been one long series of surprises. He identified her easily with her blonde hair pulled back in a high ponytail. Like her teammates, she was wearing a sleeveless vest and shorts and seated in a squat wheelchair with two large splayed wheels and a small stabiliser wheel in the centre of the back. He could see she had braces on her knees and as he watched she strapped broad Velcro bands around her ankles, knees and thighs holding them firmly together onto the chair.

When the whistle blew, the action started thick and fast immediately, with Harriet in the midst of it. It was she who scored the first goal before being tumbled by the collision with a player from the opposing team. Lucas half rose but Jimmie tugged him down as Harriet pushed with her arms to right herself and dived back into the fray. Jimmie seemed to be enjoying himself with a packet of chips, his eyes following the action.

When Harriet went for another spill landing on her back, Lucas was on the edge of his seat to see how she twisted and thrust out with her arms to spin the light-weight chair back into play.

Jimmie was laughing. "These girls play rough, but you should see the guys. They're even faster. They come on next after this match."

In the hope of seeing Harriet, he hung around through the next match and was rewarded when she appeared from the dissipating crowd in her usual chair, wearing a light tracksuit. Jimmie jogged off and returned pushing the empty sporting wheelchair with a backpack sitting on the seat. He wondered briefly who had helped her when she arrived but her casual thanks and goodbyes to a group with several able-bodied people answered the question.

Outside, Lucas took stock, trying to re-familiarise

himself with the school. Harriet directed Jimmie away from the main car park and the lad moved ahead, playing some kind of game with the wheelchair, waggling from side to side on the footpath. New buildings took up formerly open areas and for a moment he was disoriented.

The car park he felt should have been familiar, but it had been a bare patch of dirt, not this large rectangle surrounded by concrete footpaths. Her car was the only one there, in the specially paved area off to one side, designated for disability. Harriet handed her keys to Jimmie and Lucas helped him load the sporting wheelchair into the hatchback.

"It that the same tree?"

Harriet swivelled in her chair to see where he pointed. "I imagine so."

She sounded indifferent and he hesitated. "It's much bigger of course." Curiosity triumphed and he marched across the open area to the spreading tree at the far corner. How many afternoons had he waited for Harriet to come out from her classes under that tree? He expected it to be too dark to see what he was looking for, but a security light close by shone on the blotchy trunk. Scarred by the careless engravings of a multitude of students, he nevertheless looked for one particular carving.

There it was. He ran his fingers over the grooves in the timber. The bark bulged slightly around the lettering, but it was still legible.

"Did you do that?" Jimmie's voice startled him out of his preoccupation.

He looked down at the boy, seeing the brightness in the brown eyes. "Yes. I used to hang out here a long time ago and I got bored."

Jimmie traced the lettering with his finger. "L...H...4... H...E...4... e...ev..."

"Forever."

"It's in a heart. Was Harriet your girlfriend?"

"For a little while. A long time ago."

"Before the accident?"

Lucas looked across the open space to where Harriet waited. Separated from them by two gutters and a sea of loose gravel her wheelchair couldn't traverse. "Yes, before the accident." Separated from him by a whole lot more. When he'd carved those initials, he believed in forever, and he was starting to believe Harriet might have too. If only he could find out the meaning in words spoken to an outsider, overheard at a time she couldn't have known of his presence.

The lad licked his lips nervously. "Was it your motorbike?"

Lucas nodded absently, his mind distracted. Harriet had been the same age as this boy. Vulnerable. Barely more than a child. He hadn't taken that into account back then, more concerned with his own ego, his own feelings. Once again, he looked at the distance between them.

She sat quite still, her eyes lowered to her lap where her hands tangled in that nervous way she had. Not indifferent after all. But her incapacity to span the divide was more than just physical. He would have to make the first move. The question remained, did he want to?

With a last brush of his fingers over the battered relic of an innocent youth, he smiled down at the boy. "We'd better get you home."

**4**
______

"How did you get this number?" After the cool parting the other night, Harriet was in no mood to be receptive to Lucas. His interest in that old tree had raised hopes that had been cruelly dashed on his return. He'd told her he'd see her off safely and stood quietly chatting to Jimmie while she levered herself into the car. She might as well have left while he was on the other side of the car park with his new best friend. "I asked a question, Lucas. How did you get this number?"

"Geek magic of course." There was an undertone in his voice that suggested he was laughing. Like he'd done the first time he'd pulled her phone number out of thin air back when they first met.

"I suppose you Googled it somehow."

"You can't Google silent numbers. But I'll keep my secret for now. I called to invite you to dinner. We need to talk."

"I don't think we have anything to say to each other."

"Harriet, after everything that went on, the lies you told, I think you owe me this."

There was no humour in the severe statement and she

told herself she was glad. He was too disturbing to have in her life again. She'd barely survived the last time he walked away, even though it was at her instigation. "I owe you an apology, Lucas. That's all I owe you. I'm sorry I lied. There's nothing more."

"That's not good enough. I want explanations. I want to know why."

"You know why. You heard it all the other day."

"I heard part of a conversation. Don't you think I deserve better than that?"

He deserved so much more. He deserved more than she could ever give him. "I really have nothing more to say." Her throat was so tight, that last came out more as a squeak.

"Harry, come on. How hard can it be?"

"Too hard…" She slammed the receiver down just in time. Before the gasping breath gave away how close she was to tears. Tears she mustn't shed. There'd already been far too many.

The sight of Jacarandas blooming along the river as Harriet went to work the following week served as a reminder that time ruled all things. The purple flowers were dreaded by those students preparing for final exams as their blooms invariably coincided with the schedule for final assignments and exams at the end of the year and for Harriet and Lucas they had marked the final intense months of their relationship. Even seven years later the sight of the Jacarandas lovely flowers caused Harriet's throat to close and her chest to tighten. They were linked to too many memories.

Even Jimmie's cheerfulness niggled and when she was short with him over a mistake, she had to pull herself back into line. Her rudeness to Lucas on the phone haunted her. He'd been right, she did owe him at least a few minutes of her time. Being afraid didn't cut it as an excuse for poor behaviour. She'd been brought up better than that. She was better than that. But somehow Lucas triggered all her defensive mechanisms. Because he was important. It was easy to be calm and polite when you didn't care.

Lucas didn't understand what he was doing outside Harriet's office building. He spent the morning signing off on a major government contract and should have headed straight back to his office instead of making this detour. Since Harriet hung up on him he'd avoided thinking of her, filling his mind with encryption codes and long strings of numbers.

Somehow today he couldn't get her out of his mind. Looking up at the Jacaranda tree bursting into bloom he considered that maybe it was the time of year that was interfering with his concentration.

Jimmie greeted him with a simple pleasure that soothed something raw inside his chest. When several other people arrived, the young receptionist pointed him down the hallway and excused himself to deal with the newcomers. Lucas walked slowly towards Harriet's office, curious about how she would greet him after the phone episode. Reaching her door, he paused, waiting for her to notice him but she seemed oblivious to his presence.

He could see a spreadsheet up on the screen, but she just seemed to be staring at it, making no movement at all. "Harriet?"

She turned abruptly, releasing a small gasp. "Lucas, I didn't expect you. Is something wrong?" Looking at her pale face Lucas felt he should be asking the same question. Her white face only made the pink tinge around her eyes more obvious and he wondered what would make a determinedly cheerful person like Harriet cry in the workplace. "Are the computers all running okay?"

Nodding, Harriet fixed the smile back on her face, "Yes, brilliantly thank you. Everyone is thrilled. You're very popular around here at the moment."

Sitting down at the spare workstation Lucas shrugged, "Only until something goes wrong. But if it does make sure you give me a call." With a nervous laugh, Harriet shook her head. "We Googled you, so we know you are far too important to do house calls. We'll call the technician who left us his number if there are problems." There was an awkward pause and Lucas waited patiently for some reaction.

"Lucas, I'm pleased you did drop in. I wanted to apologise for hanging up on you the other day. I had no excuse for being rude." The words came out in a rush as she fixed a determined smile on her face.

"If you want to make it up to me, how about dinner. You could come over and have Spaghetti Bolognese. I still do the recipe you like." Her eyes widened and he saw the smile waver.

"What's your house like?"

He looked at the wheelchair and smiled ruefully "Not very accessible, to tell the truth. An old Queenslander on the side of a hill."

She bit her lip, forgetting to smile and Lucas watched her face, fascinated by the struggle. "You could bring the stuff to my place if you like. I have a decent kitchen." It was his turn to be surprised. He expected her to take the excuse and run with it. Now she was inviting him into her home.

Lucas stood preparing to leave, "That sounds good. Where and when? Tonight would be good for me."

Harriet gulped. So soon, but then less time to get nervous over it. Small consolation. "Sure, come any time after seven. I usually swim when I get home." It was a mistake mentioning the swimming, she realised when his eyes brightened. He'd always been a keen swimmer, using the university pool several mornings a week. "You have a pool? Would it be imposing on you if I joined you this evening?"

Harriet shook her head reluctantly. "No, of course not. It's the complex pool on the roof level. Technically it isn't supposed to be used in the evening because the indoor pool is available twenty-four seven. I have special permission and a key." She wrote down the address and told him to use the intercom so she could buzz him up when he arrived.

After Lucas left, Harriet found herself staring at the spread sheet again until she forced herself to get on with the work. At least it wasn't really a date so there was no way she would be getting the wrong idea. Just two old...friends... former lovers... former...she had to remember that, having a meal together and catching up. That was all Lucas wanted.

Even though she expected him, the buzzer still made her jump. She'd been on edge ever since Lucas made the arrangement. Pressing the downstairs entry release she moved back into the lounge area and then changed her mind, waiting in the hallway. She heard the chime of the lift and opened the door, pushing it back until it locked in place.

He was so damned tall. It had been nice when they danced all those years ago, his jaw resting on her head, her cheek against his beating heart. Now she was navel gazing, the silver buckle on his leather belt in her direct line of sight. She lifted her chin quickly, meeting his amused look. She had not been looking at the bulge in his pants. Well, only indirectly.

"Where should I put this stuff?'

"Kitchen. Straight through and on the left." He strode past her, shopping bags in one hand and a canvas backpack in the other. Closing the door, she followed him to the kitchen. He'd shed his jacket somewhere but otherwise he was still dressed as he'd been at her office. The scruff shadowing his jaw-line somehow only made him seem sexier. Like morning after stubble. She'd never stayed the whole night so she hadn't really seen him like that.

The relationship hadn't really progressed that far back then. Going home each night to comply with her parent's curfew made sure of that, but now she could imagine how he must have looked, all ruffled and prickly. There must be a special clipper to keep it at that short length. Not something she'd ever thought about before.

She joined him in the kitchen as he put a pack of minced beef in the fridge and dropped the rest of the shopping onto the long granite bench. "You must be planning on feeding an army."

"There's something for dessert as well."

"You've developed a sweet tooth?"

"I always had one, but the budget didn't run to fancy stuff while I was studying."

He pulled out a frozen cheesecake and pot of French vanilla ice-cream and put them in fridge and freezer respectively. "I think I remember you liked raspberry cheesecake."

Startled at him remembering something so

inconsequential she almost dropped the carton of juice she was putting away. He scooped it from her failing grip and tucked it on the shelf beside her bottle of milk. "Hold on. I've got this."

Embarrassed, she lashed out. "I'm perfectly capable of putting shopping away. It's my legs not my hands."

"Hey, cool it. I wasn't implying anything. It's all done now anyway." He loomed over her, hands on hips and a crease between his dark brows. "Still Miss Independence, I see."

A reluctant smile twitched her lips. "You remember all my bad points."

"Raspberry cheesecake couldn't be called a bad point."

"It's a weakness all the same."

He brushed her cheek with his knuckles in a playful gesture that tightened something in her chest. "So? Nobody's perfect."

Picking up his backpack he moved out of the kitchen. "Now, where can I get changed? I don't imagine you want me stripping off in your living room."

She contemplated his crooked grin and let her gaze run down his body. *Well...* "Of course not. You can use the spare bedroom. I'll show you."

With a quick twirl of her wheels, she led the way to the bedrooms. "This one. If you need anything, I'll be just across the hall."

With a questioning glance towards the door of the master bedroom, he nodded. "I'll yell if I need help." Not that help was what he needed from her.

"You..." He was so infuriatingly attractive like this. Shaking her head, she entered her own room, pushing the door to with unnecessary vigour so the slam echoed down the corridor. *What was happening to her?* He was waking up things, things better left buried, dormant.

By the time she changed, he was well and truly ready, back in the kitchen slicing onions. The overhead lights gave his light, honey-brown skin a glow as it stretched over strong shoulders and accentuated the well-developed pectorals and washboard abs. Two, four, six...all accounted for. A fine trickle of dark hair bisected his stomach below his navel, drawing attention to his masculinity.

Was fate cruel or kind sending Lucas into her life, wearing nothing but a low-cut pair of designer swimming shorts? Not really budgie smugglers, more like...what was bigger than a budgie? A galah, maybe a cockatoo? She wiped the silly grin off her face as he looked up inquiringly.

"I just thought I'd get a head start while I was waiting."

His eyes flicked over her, taking in the hair up in a topknot and the plum coloured loose jacket covering her matching bikini. The way his eyes darkened as they lingered on the flesh revealed by the opening of the coat did something funny to her pulse. She saw him stiffen as he took a good look at the smooth, flesh coloured fibre-glass knee braces. The warmth seeped away at the sudden crease between his brows. He was like all the rest, forgetting she was a woman because of her legs. Wrapping her arms around her body she tilted her chin, daring him to say something.

She was doing it again. He'd seen the interest in her eyes as they lingered on his chest and lower. But as soon as she'd seen him checking her out she closed up, her eyes chilly and mouth compressed. He'd learned about body language in an extracurricular course at UCLA and the folded arms were classic.

Something was going on but how did he get her to tell him what he'd done to upset her? It was too easy to say the wrong thing. Especially with their history. All the same, it was surprisingly easy to fall back into the old patterns. From before everything went wrong. Grabbing a clean tea-towel from the drawer, he spread it over the chopped onions. "All ready to cook when we get back."

"How did you know where everything was?"

"By being a nosey parker. I was looking for a board to cut the onions on and I think I must have opened every cupboard in the place before I found it."

She moved away, the glide of the wheelchair smoothly skirting the furniture. Not that there was a great deal in the starkly black and white room. The dining setting, a couple of large couches facing the wide screen television, a coffee table or two and what looked to be a mechanical armchair similar to one his mother had in the nursing home to help her get up.

Waiting for him at the door, a towel bunched on her lap, he was reminded again of how different it was relating to someone in a wheelchair. He had a mate in the U.S. in a wheelchair, a brilliant researcher, but his was a fancy motorised thing that could raise and lower so he could bring himself up to the level of the conversation. Harriet seemed to spend a lot of time either staring at his midriff or craning her neck to look up at his face. "Doing anything special for your birthday?"

She reached over to press the up button for the lift. "Just dinner with Mum and Dad, I imagine. They might do a cake for morning tea at work."

In a few weeks, she would be twenty-five. Still young,

though she didn't really act young, or dress it. He wondered what happened to all her flowy dresses and the pretty jewelled flowers she used to wear in her hair. "Did you get a big party for your twenty-first?" He'd gone with her to her cousin's shindig, held at the Hilton in the city, only a couple of weeks before they broke up.

Turning to face him in the lift she shrugged. "No. It wasn't worth it. As it turned out I was in hospital."

"Why? Were you sick?" His heart did something weird at the thought of her in hospital again. Surely, she'd been through enough with the accident.

"Not sick. Just follow up surgery on my knees."

"What sort of thing? Did something go wrong?"

"Just adding a few nuts and bolts. I doubt if I could get onto a plane without setting off the alarms, with all the metal in my legs."

"Don't you know?"

"No. I haven't been anywhere to test it."

"You were going to Noumea with your parents just after I last spoke to you."

"It didn't work out. I've been in Brisbane all this time." She slanted a wry smile up at him. "If you'd been looking."

No, he hadn't been looking. Not the first few years. But she'd been on his mind. Imagining her on the beach, at university, at parties. Dancing. He followed her from the lift, distracted by the sparkle of the swimming pool under the clear night sky.

Scattered lamps on poles added a soft glow to the surrounds but the still water was lit totally from below, clear as crystal against the sky-blue tiles. She shed her robe on a lounger by the stairs into the pool and pulled herself up with the chrome railing, steadying herself. All his imaginings had been way off the mark. And another lie exposed. Had there been any truth at all that day?

Pounding his way up and down the pool he tried to drown out the conviction that she'd been lying for a very specific purpose. What had she said to Grae? Or had Grae said it? She couldn't have joined him in the U.S. in a wheelchair. Even after she recovered from the initial trauma.

The job she had lined up near the university where his research gig was based depended on her being fit and active. And they'd both been right on one count. At the time, he wouldn't have gone without her. Not if he'd known the extent of her injuries. They'd made promises, commitments.

He slowed at the tightness in his chest, needing oxygen. He'd given it all away so easily. Hadn't even bothered to fight for it. Walking away from a girl tied to a hospital bed with horrific injuries. Even though she'd lied about it, he should have queried it. Not just taken his wounded ego to the other side of the world. No wonder she thought so little of him. Thought he wouldn't have what it takes to be with someone in a wheelchair. Gasping for breath, he stood, waist deep in the shallow lap pool.

Harriet felt rather than heard Lucas stop swimming. The sudden cessation of the backwash as he ploughed past her, his powerful body cleaving the water at speeds she couldn't hope to emulate even if her legs had been functional. She bobbed her head up when she reached the end of the pool only to find him a couple of meters away. His hair was slicked over his skull and beads of water trickled from it down his spine. Once upon a time she would have traced the flow of those droplets, right down to water level where they vanished in the plumber's cleavage of his low-cut swimmers.

He looked every bit as good as she remembered and more, the broader shoulders accentuating the narrow waist and hips, the tight butt and the long, long legs illuminated by the inset lights on the floor of the pool. She sank a little lower as her breasts tingled, afraid of him seeing the betraying hardness of her nipples under the thin bikini top.

There were too many memories. That's why she didn't have this reaction with anyone else. Her body, evil traitor, wanted all that Lucas had once offered. Her mind knew it would never work. She'd seen it too often among her friends, even relatives. Relationships were hard enough without adding the complications of a disability.

While she watched, he raked his long fingers through his hair, dragging it away from his face as he turned to face her. From the front, he was even better. She had to stop herself counting his abs again. It's not like they were hamsters and likely to multiply. The water swirled around his hips, but she could see the bulge, impressive despite the influence of the cold water.

She remembered that too, shivering as heat pooled low in her abdomen. He'd been the man who took her virginity, so of course her body felt a connection. There was nothing magical about it, whatever she believed at the time. She had to make herself believe it, or she was doomed.

His eyes gleamed vivid emerald in the reflected light from the pool and she watched, fascinated as the pupils dilated, blackness swamping the green. He'd seen her looking at him again. She licked her lips and something flared into life, his lids suddenly drooping, thick lashes shadowing his gaze. *Desire?*

"Are we finished?"

She nodded mutely, though it felt more like something was starting. She hadn't quite made it to her usual twenty laps but tonight was different. She edged her way to the steps, but he beat her there, his long stride taking him out of the water with ease. Standing on the second top step he turned and stretched out his hands. "Let me help."

Harriet stood at the bottom of the steps, her body and mind at war. It was just an offer to help. But if she touched him, the powder keg of her body's reactions would explode. She ached to touch him, but not just his hands. Could she stop herself, once she felt that first contact? *How had she come to this?* A couple of weeks ago she'd been congratulating herself on how well she was coping. Smug in her body's indifference to that side of life. Envisaging a future without a man, children, and physical passion.

Straining for first contact, her body won the battle. Her hands reached up, glided over his palms to grasp his wrist for better purchase. Long fingers wrapped around her forearms, a jellyfish burn on her skin, searing through the damp outer flesh to heat the blood in her veins to boiling point. She saw him stare at her breasts, feeling the scalding heat translate into a rosy blush that travelled from her chest to envelop her whole body. Perspiration dampened her upper lip and she ran her tongue over it, tasting the salt.

"Have you been with anyone since the accident?" He bit his bottom lip, as if he wanted to bite back the words. Too late. It was out there. Blunt as ever. That hadn't changed.

His voice was rough, urgent and she cringed. *Oh help. Was she so transparent?* She wanted to sink back into the water and drown but his hands held her, forcing her to stay, unable to escape from his probing look.

She twisted in his hold, trying to match his stare. "If this is where we play the 'I've had more lovers than you,' game I'm conceding defeat. You win."

Sheer surprise must have aided her because his grip loosened, allowing her to drop back into the pool. She'd turn into a prune before she attempted to get past him.

"Hold on a minute."

Strong arms scooped her up, dragging her back to the stairs. A muscular forearm made a rigid bar under her breasts and his other hand splayed across her stomach, pulling her against his body, dropping them both back onto the steps. Heat flared again as the curve of her bottom came in contact with his erection. It had to be memory for him too. He couldn't want her now.

All skin and muscle and breakable, useless legs. No way could she wrap them around his waist as he entered her, holding him tight like she'd done that last night together. Their first and last time. Forget kneeling over his body, on the floor in front of him as she...

His hand cupped her mound over the bikini bottoms to drag her onto his lap and she bucked, trying to get away from the sensory overload but it only ground her buttocks against him.

"Sh..ugar. Stop doing that. Geeze, Harry."

She stilled immediately at the raw tone. "Let me go, then. What are you doing?" His hand moved away, the fresh contact with the water chilling the fabric against her sensitive skin.

"Trying to hold a conversation. And don't go into shock. I told you I've been practicing."

She wondered who with and pushed the thought away. It was too painful. "What are we supposed to talk about? I'm not comparing notes."

"That's not what I meant. No-one wins if that's the way the game is played."

"Why else would you ask?"

"I'm making a mess of this. As usual. I wanted to ask... what I meant was...can you? Did the accident...effect more than your legs."

She sank into his lap, shocked and more than a little moved. He sounded like he cared. Why would it matter to him? The hard length of him still pressed between the cheeks of her bottom. Was he going to offer it? As some kind of compensation?

"Technically I'm fine...with that side of things. It's just with my legs. Awkward, much. Who would want to?"

"So, even though you can, there's been no-one?"

Why did he sound so pleased? Some kind of man thing where he staked his claim, left the flag flying and then went off to new discoveries with the assumption that his conquered lands would remain his even if he didn't want them? Although, the twitch from his erection suggested he wouldn't be averse to revisiting.

Pride came to her rescue. Belatedly. "It's none of your business." A little curt but what did he expect. Hopefully he wouldn't feel the urge to share details of his last seven years.

He stiffened, his arm tight across her midriff. A whisper of warm breath trickled across her cheek. Her skin prickled, and heat pooled low in her gut.

"I'm going to kiss you, Harry, speak now or forever hold your peace." She was lost as his mouth claimed hers, his tongue sweeping away any resistance as it savoured her lips, delving deeper to dance with hers, tasting of chlorine, of him and the sorrows born of years apart. She could taste the sadness, salt amidst the sweet, a remembered surge of timeless ecstasy, a shattering of her soul that breeched the carefully built barriers in waves of pleasure mixed with tears.

Tears that Lucas kissed away, licking the moisture from the corners of her mouth. "Enough talk."

The irony of his rueful statement triggered a bubble of something. *Happiness?* Had she forgotten happiness? No, she was happy at work. She enjoyed a joke and could laugh on demand. But this, this was more like...joy. She laughed, a wobbly sound that sounded odd. Had she lost the capacity to laugh simply for the sake of it? Her memory failed her. How did you tell the difference? When you'd been living a lie for so long.

5

He couldn't be sure at first if it were Harriet trembling or his own reaction that caused the surface of the water to ripple out from their linked bodies. Curled into him, she shivered convulsively so he carefully adjusted his hold and lifted her from the water. He'd come close to the edge himself, his legs were not that great, but she was such a lightweight, he hardly noticed. Her breath cooled his collarbone, still wet from her hair.

"Do I put you straight into the chair or do you need to stand up to dry yourself?"

"If you let me stand, I'll put my robe on before I sit down. Then I can dry my legs."

The huskiness of her voice told the tale and the flush across her cheekbones when he finally caught a glimpse of her face caught at his throat. Embarrassment or anger? Either way he could be in trouble. He helped her with the coat and eased her down onto her wheelchair.

"Thanks. Could you pass me the towel?"

He shook his head, smiling, "Let me do it." He squatted in front of her, resting on one knee. "Please."

She returned his gaze, her brows drawn together. "Why?"

"I want to." He gently wrapped the towel around her calf. "Tell me if I'm doing anything wrong."

Dragging his eyes away from the puzzled expression on her face, he dried her legs carefully, patting the skin revealed by the cut-outs of the braces. He could see scarring above and below the moulded supports and a glimpse of ugly puckered scars across each of her exposed knees. He would have to persuade her to let him see them properly. Now he knew more of what she'd been through, he needed to understand, to see the extent of the damage.

With a final pat of her foot he looked up at her, relieved to see the angry flush had faded a little. "How's that?"

"Fine. Better than I usually do. I have trouble reaching between my toes." She frowned as she wiggled the toes in question and he tweaked one with a broad grin, to be rewarded with a soft chuckle. "Stirrer."

He stood and reached for his own towel. "Shall we go eat?"

"Yes, please. I'm famished." She blushed at his knowing look and he silently breathed a sigh of relief. One hurdle crossed. It could have ruined everything, but so far so good. He hadn't thought it through when he'd held her, touched her. The feel of her in his arms had blown his mind. So much so he'd even forgotten that long-ago conversation where she'd broken everything he'd thought they had. Even now, he wasn't sure if even that betrayal couldn't be explained away. Because if everything she'd said that day was true, she wouldn't have responded to his lovemaking.

He would have liked to follow her into the master suite, to see how she handled changing. Instead he returned to her spare bedroom and swiftly dressed so he could get started on the meal. By the time she returned, wearing an oversized pink T-shirt dress that came halfway down her thighs he already had the onions and mince browning and a large pot of water on the gas cook-top.

She gathered cutlery and plates, balancing them on her lap. "Would you like to eat on the balcony?"

"Sure thing."

"You sounded very American when you said that."

"I was there nearly six years and it's an easy accent to pick up."

"I wish..." She turned away to set the glass topped table on the balcony and he watched her manoeuvre around the small space with elegant precision. He wished she'd come too. Had been angry with her for so long, for staying behind. She would have loved the house at Malibu, overlooking the beach. Plenty of room for her to get around and mostly accessible.

"How long were you in hospital?"

Her head jerked up from arranging the cutlery. "Eight months."

In an era where people were being kicked out two days after major surgery, it didn't sound probable. "All at once or were you back and forth for follow up surgery?"

Coming back inside she gathered up the wine glasses. "Eight months initially, although some of that was in rehab. The follow ups were only a few days each time and some day-surgery."

"How many times?"

"A few. I don't remember."

Or don't want to tell. He turned away to pick up a clean spoon. "Do you want to taste the Bolognese?"

After a momentary hesitation, she approached, placing the wheelchair at a slight angle to bring her closer and he held the spoon to her lips. This was an old routine and he wondered if she would play along.

Licking her lips, she smiled, and it was the old smile he remembered. "It tastes the same."

"A fahmilee recipee brought over from Eetaly by my Grandmama." She giggled at his atrocious Italian accent and he put out his hand to swipe a smidgen of sauce from the corner of her mouth with his thumb, holding it up so she could see. "Waste not, want not."

Obediently she opened her mouth and he dipped his thumb into the warmth, her lips closing just above the knuckle. Her tongue wrapped around the tip, cleaning it of the sauce and he drew a sharp breath at the erotic vision of her gazing up at him while sucking on his thumb. He shifted uncomfortably as blood surged south again. They'd been young and inexperienced when they first met. Harriet had been just a kid. They'd thought they had all the time in the world to learn each other.

Reluctantly he withdrew his thumb, bringing it to his own mouth, wanting to taste her. With a low exclamation, Harriet swivelled away, opening the fridge. "What shall we drink? I have red or white if you want wine."

"Red would be better with Bolognese."

She closed the fridge and vanished down the hallway and he turned back to check the spaghetti. He knew the decision he'd made was the right one. It was Harriet's reaction he wasn't sure about. No matter what she believed about his lack of staying power, he wanted to take a chance. The strong physical pull appeared to be the only weak spot in her armour. He could work with that. It was a known factor.

For a man who preferred a trial by numbers approach, letting his body do the talking had its drawbacks. With

Harriet, nothing ever worked the way he expected. It had been a major part of her attraction. The fairy queen and the numbers geek. However unlikely, it had worked until the accident. He'd never made the same connection with anyone before or since.

Settled on the balcony, wine on the table and plates piled high with the spaghetti Bolognese, he took a moment to admire the view. "I see why you like it." He prodded at his plate with the cutlery, suddenly nervous. "The views from my place are nearly as good. It needs a lot of work." He glanced over at Harriet in her wheelchair. More than he initially thought. "I'm thinking of putting a lap pool downstairs. It's the one thing I miss from my apartment building."

She looked up from twirling the pasta around her fork. "How big is this place?"

"Two levels. The main part is upstairs which is big enough, but the underneath is enclosed as well. Just for storage and a laundry but they did it with stone external walls so it's quite solid. I'm thinking a pool and gym and an entertainment area. It could open up to the back yard for barbeques."

"Do you do a lot of entertaining?"

"Not at the moment. But once...once the renovations are done, I might do more."

"It sounds awfully big for a man on his own." She froze, her fork halfway to her mouth, trailing strands of spaghetti. A ruddy stain marred her cheeks and she looked...almost guilty. For a moment he thought she might mention the past, about... "I forgot, you have a girlfriend."

He wanted to swear but he had to control himself. It was like the weekend one of his Californian colleagues took him on a canoe trek in one of their national parks. There'd been a faun, just like the one in that movie he saw as a kid. They'd tried to get close, to take a photo but it skittered away every time. "You mean Angela? The woman in Jimmie's newspaper?"

"She's very beautiful."

"She is. But we don't live together, if that's what you want to know."

"It's none of my business."

He watched her stabbing at the plate and suppressed a smile. "It could be."

Her startled response and quick shake of the head made him want to throttle her. Or himself. Was she being deliberately obtuse? Maybe he was jumping the gun. But he wanted her. Physically, anyway. The other stuff he needed to figure out. He wouldn't be trusting her with his feelings any time soon. "Why not, Harry? Give me one good reason."

"It just wouldn't work. I just know. I'm just not interested in anything like that."

"That's a lot of 'justs'. Don't tell me you *just* aren't interested in the sex, Harriet. Even you aren't that good a liar."

"That's different."

"How different?"

"It would be just..." She flushed at his snorted response. "All right, it would be simply sex. Just...simply...I mean." Throwing down her fork she glared at him. "People like me don't get to have long term relationships."

"You're wrong, I know several guys in wheelchairs who are happily married for the long term. A couple even have children."

"I bet their wives are their carers too. I bet none of them have high powered careers."

"You'd be wrong. Yes, a couple are like that, but not all."

"It must be the exception that proves the rule. I know for a fact how hard it is."

"Then tell me. I expect data, statistics. Convince me."

"I don't have statistics, but I do have empiric data. Like the girls I play basketball with. Three of them were in relationships when they were injured, and their boyfriends didn't hang around."

"That only proves they weren't the right men. Did any of them dump their boyfriends after the accident?"

"They...I don't know." She stared back at him and he knew the message went home. She took a deep breath. "I could send you information, research that shows strains on families with a child with a disability or severe illness result in a higher level of family breakdown."

"I'll take your word for it. All the same, it doesn't mean you should write off any chance of a relationship. How do you know the relationships you mention would have lasted, even without the complications of one of them having a disability of having a child with a disability?"

Her temper flared, sparking her eyes and flagging her cheeks with colour. "I don't. But I know my parents nearly divorced."

"Jack and Caro? I can't imagine it."

Harriet shifted her gaze to her glass of wine. How did she get out of this one if he asked for more information? She didn't want to talk about her childhood. Hopefully he would assume it was recently.

His brows were drawn together as he scanned her face. "Seriously? They seem devoted."

"They are. They managed to get over it. It doesn't always have anything to do with how much you love each other."

She saw his mouth twist, drawing down the harsh lines. "That at least I can understand." Her stomach turned over as he continued. "But parents of a child are one thing. I imagine there is a level of anxiety for any parent. Why should a couple who know what they're getting into be at risk?"

"All kinds of things. Going out becomes a pain. Some restaurants say they are accessible but if you want to use the toilets they aren't. There is also the intimacy thing. Having to help your lover go to the bathroom pretty much wrecks any romance."

"You need help to go to the toilet?"

"Not usually. But sometimes if my knees are playing up, I need help to move from the chair onto the pedestal."

"So, you reckon that if I get to see you pee it will destroy our relationship?"

Flushing, she evaded his sceptical gaze. "Yes…No…It's just an example. It's about being a carer instead of a husband. It changes the dynamic."

He looked at her for a long moment. "I suppose it does." The finality in his tone ended the subject as he poured more wine.

She should be pleased she'd managed to shut him up. But Harriet didn't feel any satisfaction. She sipped at the wine, puzzled at her own reaction. She'd wanted to convince him, didn't she? She shouldn't feel disappointed when he accepted it. He'd go away now and cut the last ties and she wouldn't have to be reminded, wouldn't have to feel guilty about the things she should have done but somehow never had. Because she hadn't wanted to lose that final connection?

"So, what about friendship?" He waved his wine glass in the air and she wondered how much he'd had. The bottle was only half empty, so not much. "We could be friends with benefits. Isn't that the latest fashion?"

Quick recovery much, and what was with the peculiar smile? "I don't get it"

"You say you can't do relationships because they will inevitably crash and burn under the circumstances. What about friendships?"

Was it a trick question? "Friends would be all right."

"How do you feel about us being friends?"

"Is that even possible? You hated me not so long ago."

"I could give you an orgasm. That's the act of a true friend in my opinion."

"You have such an ego."   .

"No thanks to you."

He was right. She'd cut him down ruthlessly at their final meeting. She shouldn't have been surprised he never came back. Even though she'd wanted him to overrule her, to demand the truth, to stay with her through all those miserable months. Like she wanted him to overrule her now, demand they start again. Push aside her reservations and make her believe that for them, it could work. It would be nice to pretend, for a little while that it could work. That love would be enough.

"Harriet, I'm serious."

"It wouldn't work."

"Couldn't we try?"

"What about Angela?"

"She's a work colleague, we aren't in a relationship."

Harriet wondered what that meant. Was she a 'colleague with benefits'? They looked like more than friends in the photo. But she could hardly blame him for sleeping with other women. She'd sent him away. It wasn't until her best friend from school visited the hospital after the breakup that she realised what sending him away could mean. But the thought of him going out with Sondra, gorgeous titian haired Sondra who'd always fancied Lucas, just about sent her crazy. She'd told the redhead the most atrocious lies about Lucas, yet the girl had still pursued him. He encouraged her too, all the way to the States.

"I don't know, Lucas. I didn't expect this."

One eyebrow quirked upwards. "It's not that you object to me pawing you? Mauling you? Fumbling around like a dork who didn't know what to do."

"What?" *How did he know?* "Sondra told you what I said?"

"No, Harriet, my little deceiver, I heard you telling her."

"You were there, at the hospital, that day?"

"Fool that I was I thought maybe I should come and see you. I wondered if you'd been out to it on painkillers that day and didn't know what you were saying."

"You came back?" He hadn't abandoned her without a second thought. She suppressed the surge of joy that bubbled up. That was then.

"Yes. But I didn't appreciate the comment about my pencil dick. That at least I recognised as a lie. Why the hell would you want to humiliate me in front of your friends?"

"Not all my friends. Only Sondra."

His brows had drawn so close together they were almost one line. "Why Sondra in particular?"

"Because she told me she was going to shag you." She was almost yelling, and she fought to bring her voice under control. "Because she told me she'd been waiting for us to break up because she knew you had a thing for her."

"And you didn't want me to shag her?"

"No. But it didn't make any difference did it. You still took her to the U.S. with you instead of me."

She sucked in a gasping breath. There seemed to be no oxygen in the air. The screech of the metal chair across the tiles grated like fingernails on a blackboard as Lucas came to kneel beside her. "Look at me. Harriet, look at me. What's wrong, what can I do?" His eyes captured hers, ferocious in their intensity. Her chest eased immediately. She clutched at his hand, squeezing it as her breathing deepened. "Is it asthma?"

Shaking her head, she kept her grip on his hand. His other hand rubbed her back, bringing him closer. "Garlic breath." It came out in a wheeze, but he heard it and laughed.

"Pot...kettle." He kissed her, lightly, on the corner of her mouth. Maybe it would be possible. For a little while. Until he realised how much it would limit his life. Until then. She released his hand and he moved away, standing in a graceful movement she envied. "Shall we adjourn to the interior my faerie queen?"

"Don't call me that."

"Very well, my lady." He bowed low with a flourish and a wicked grin. "I'll bring this stuff in while you go and start on dessert."

Safe inside, Harriet found some bowls and spoons. It was like riding a roller coaster. One minute he was all chilly or stormy and aggressive, the next he was laughing, just like the old Lucas. Which could she believe? Or were they all real? Was he as confused about his emotions as she was?

Piling the dishes in the sink, Lucas seemed very much at home. "I like the layout of this kitchen. Plenty of room without having to trek to Nepal to reach things."

"Since when did you become a kitchen aficionado?"

"I'm renovating remember. I think you'll like my house. Remember the Jacarandas on the street outside my old digs? This place has them too."

She remembered well enough. The streetlight behind them sent a lavender glow into his louvered veranda bedroom. With the deep green and gold embroidered quilt it had made the room an enchanted place.

At his insistence, they both sat on the soft leather couch to eat the cheesecake, his legs and elbows brushing against hers as they ate. He talked about his work and, hungry for information, she sat rapt, watching his mobile face come alive with enthusiasm. "So, it was the security software that you were working on for your masters that started you off?"

"Yes. The government agencies were all over it. They didn't have that deep level of encryption on what they were using. From there it just mushroomed."

Which meant it had all been worth it. His hands shaped dreams as he talked, describing fresh fields to conquer and new visions to pursue. She couldn't go there, because she would be a lead weight, slowing him down. But for a little while perhaps she could taste something of what he'd become before drawing the line in the sand.

"Am I boring you?" His voice was serious, but he smiled down at her.

"Never."

Emerald eyes searched her face. "Can I believe it?"

"Of course you can. I never lied about my interest in what you do."

The frown creased his brow and she wanted to smooth it away. "It's hard to remember what was true and what wasn't anymore."

"Does it matter?"

"I don't know. I know this matters." He swooped to kiss

her, catching her with the last mouthful of cheesecake. Hastily she swallowed as he lifted his head to examine her face. "Yes. This matters."

He took the plate and spoon from her limp hold and placed them on the coffee table. Fascinated, she let him slide his arm under her legs to turn her onto his lap, careful not to jar her. It was as if he knew already how easily an unwary movement could damage her knees.

To have his strong arms around her again was almost unbearable. Her heart immediately signalled readiness for what must follow, thumping heavily behind her ribcage. His fingers pressed lightly against her collarbone and tracked a trail of heat up the side of her neck until he cupped her cheek with his palm. The first touch of his mouth almost didn't register, a faint whisper, more breath than skin, across her lower lip. A nip of teeth, then, followed by soothing tongue and the pressure to open, to welcome him in.

From there she fell into sensation, a vortex of moist warmth and taste, accompanied by the stroking of a large hand over her body, teasing a nipple, massaging the whole before moving down. Down to the bare skin of her leg, a soft squeeze and then gliding up the muscle...Time spun out of control as she delved under fine silk to do a recount of those abs and brush softly over flat nipples, pinching them into miniature peaks. Time...the alarm? Ringing. Ringing. She dragged herself back to reality. "The phone."

"Leave it, they'll ring back." He kissed her again, a long drugging kiss that made everything fade.

Struggling from his hold she shook her head to clear it. "No, I have to answer."

He lifted her into the wheelchair and she zipped across the room to grab the cordless phone, turning away as she answered it, slightly breathless. *Who on earth was so darned important?* She spoke quickly and low, so he couldn't hear. Meanwhile, his dick was just about jumping out of his jocks. He tried to adjust it with the heel of his hand without much success, so he stood and undid his fly.

"Put that away."

She looked sexy as hell with her hair all rumpled, and mouth swollen from his kisses, but the somnolence had gone from her eyes leaving them a brittle blue.

"Hey, you were with me, sweetheart."

"My dad will be here in about seven minutes and I don't want him walking in to find that...thing...hanging out."

*Crap.* "Your dad? What's going on?" Hanging out was an exaggeration, it was still confined, mostly, by his jocks. He tucked himself away as neatly as he could and zipped his pants, tucking his shirt in. Vengeful fathers had the advantage of deflating...things.

"I couldn't convince them there was nothing wrong because I was out of breath. He insisted on coming over to check. So, pack up your stuff and get out of here."

"I'm not leaving. I'm not afraid to face your father."

"Why should you be afraid? I don't want to have to explain your presence. That's all."

"Why shouldn't I be afraid? I'm the lout who had his daughter out on a motorcycle in the middle of the night. If it weren't for that..." He waved vaguely in the direction of her wheelchair.

"No-one blames you for that, Lucas. It was an accident."

"It was my fault we were on the road. I insisted on taking you home."

"I know. But you were right. They would have worried if

I didn't go home. If we're going to apportion blame, what about the time we wasted while I argued. If we'd left when you wanted to, that truck wouldn't have been there, we wouldn't have been there."

"You were still my responsibility and I didn't take care of you."

Her face softened. "Lucas, you always looked after me." She manoeuvred the chair closer, reaching up to take his hand. Her fingers were swallowed by his, large and warm and comforting. "No-one could have looked after me better, been more caring. You respected my parent's wishes which a lot of guys your age might not have."

Apart from marrying their daughter without letting them know. Having sex with her. And look how that turned out. "Until the day of the accident. I didn't look after you properly then."

"That was my choice, Lucas. And you came back. Even after I told you to go. I wish I'd known."

"I wish..." The beep as someone used the card entry on the door distracted him. "Your father has a key?"

"You really didn't think they'd let their disabled daughter manage on her own. They live in the apartment block second along the street from here. That was about as far as the umbilical cord would stretch."

"Seriously? You let your parents make those kinds of decisions for you?" It didn't sound like her. She'd always been independent before. Almost too much so.

"There are reasons. Sometimes you have to compromise." There was a shadow in her eyes as if memories haunted them.

She was smoothing her hair as Jack Emerson entered the room, his eyes, so reminiscent of Harriet's, going straight to the visitor.

"Well, well. Lucas Hall. What a blast from the past."

Harriet grimaced behind her father's back as she rolled her eyes and he had to smile. "That's exactly what Harriet said when I walked into her office. Hello, Jack." He extended his hand and after a momentary hesitation the older man gripped it.

"What brings you to this part of the world? I understand you've been in the U.S. all this time."

"I've been back in Australia around twelve months. The government offered some very favourable terms to move my company back here."

"Twelve months." The glance he gave his daughter was worried, but she returned it with that fixed smile.

"His company donated a new computer system, Dad. He came over for dinner, so we could catch up on the gossip. It's been a while."

With a thoughtful look that encompassed both of them her father nodded. "Seven years. A lot can happen in seven years."

For a man in his early sixties, he looked older. Careworn. The pale hair like Harriet's flecked with silver. The cost to the family had been high. Lucas took the hint. "Look, I'll just get my things together and head off."

Harriet didn't look all that pleased but Jack looked relieved as Lucas entered the hallway. Minutes later, bag in hand, he paused as he left the bedroom to judge what stage the conversation was at. Jack's voice carried clearly. "After all that's happened, what are you doing having dinner with him?"

"It's only a catch-up dinner. Simple, Dad. We bumped into each other at work, we were curious about each other's lives over the last seven years and we had dinner to talk about it. Isn't it natural? We were good friends for a while back then. We probably won't even see each other again after this."

Lucas felt his throat tighten. *Good friends wasn't half of it, Harriet Emerson.* He wasn't finished with her by any stretch of the imagination. Jack Emerson obviously didn't know the half of it either. Another lie on Harriet's part. Or an omission. Which came to the same thing.

"Just remember what happened last time, Harriet, that's all I ask." Jack's voice was pleading, and Lucas found that the most disturbing thing of all about the conversation.

When he first dated Harriet, Jack had taken him under his wing. It had been a revelation after his own dysfunctional family life, to be absorbed into Harriet's small family. He'd been eleven when his father died and not much older when his siblings left home, driven away by the bitter recriminations of their mother. Caro was difficult at times but there was no doubting her love for Jack and Harriet. He never really found out why she was occasionally moody. The only explanation had been an offhand comment about a nervous condition. He could understand her reservations about him dating her daughter. That's why he'd tried so hard to comply with their rules and made sure she was home every night.

Closing the bedroom door firmly he heard the sudden silence as they registered his imminent return. "I'll just finish cleaning up in the kitchen," he announced as he put his backpack on one of the kitchen stools. Jack nodded, but Harriet's face was unreadable with the fixed smile she was wearing for her father's benefit. It only took a few minutes and Harriet dried up and put away. Jack waited at the doorway to the hall, studiously looking at his blackberry as if to give them an illusion of privacy. Now was his chance.

"I should have told you earlier, about Sondra."

Harriet hung the tea towel over the handle of the oven. "You don't have to tell me, Lucas."

"I think you have a right to know this." He glanced over at her father before fixing his gaze on her upturned face. "I sold Sondra the spare ticket. I needed the money."

"Sold it to her? But she said...What about the bike?"

"A write off. The insurance didn't cover anything like what I would have got selling it."

"So that's why you had to sell my ticket. To make up the difference."

"I didn't see her after we landed."

"You went with her to Vegas. She sent me a photo."

"I went to a convention for work. Vegas is a major conference centre. She was working there, and we bumped into each other. She latched onto the group of guys I was with. You probably saw the movie. A group of guys, a lot of booze, a few willing women."

"I bet she was willing..."

He barely heard the mutter, but he leaned closer. "I wasn't." She stared, and he put a finger to her chin, lifting her jaw to shut her gaping mouth. "Catching flies?"

Jack pocketed his phone with a gruff goodnight to his daughter. "I'd better get back. Caro will be wondering what's keeping me."

Lucas nodded. "And worrying, I suppose."

"It's what parents do."

Once in the lift going down, Lucas turned to Jack. "You should know, I had no idea Harriet hadn't made a full recovery after the accident."

The older man smiled tiredly. "I know, son. I remember what she said she told you at the time."

A curious turn of phrase. "What did happen after I left? Did something go wrong? Was there some damage that wasn't picked up at the time?"

Stepping out of the lift, Jack moved to one side and Lucas followed. "Whatever she may have told you when she saw you, the fact is that Harriet knew from the first night before they even took her into surgery that she would never walk normally again."

"How could they be so sure?"

Jack rubbed his chin as if debating what to say. "I suppose now you know the truth there's no harm in telling you the details. Her knees and the bones in her legs were totally shattered and all the ligaments were either snapped or crushed. She has enough metal in her to rebuild the Storey Bridge holding what's left of the bones together, but the repaired ligaments will never have the strength to support the joints."

"Is there nothing else they can do?"

"This is the best they can do. When Harriet spoke to you, even that was considered unlikely. They wanted to amputate both legs completely. Harriet refused and we supported her. If we'd known what it would cost her at the time, I doubt we would have done the same."

"Surely keeping her legs was the best possible thing for her."

"One swift operation and learning to walk on prosthetics as opposed to thirteen operations and a lifetime of pain? I don't think so. But it was her choice. She was eighteen, so it was up to her."

With a strangled groan, Lucas sat on the couch opposite the lifts. He'd seen it, that first moment when she'd stood, the sharp breath, the perspiration beading on her upper lip and forehead as she shuffled her way to the wheelchair. The tension that came from being in pain.

Jack sat beside him. "You really did care about her, didn't you?"

"You knew my position. I was upfront with you right from the start, Jack."

"I know. It worries me. Because I know what Harriet's feelings were. I wonder whether any of us did the right thing."

"It's not too late to fix some things."

The faded blue eyes sharpened and Lucas kept his gaze steady. With a shrug, the older man turned away. "We shall see."

**6**

_______

She couldn't believe it. Maybe the thing about Sondra. It had the ring of truth, knowing her former friend. But Lucas, back in her life for however long. That was something she'd consigned to dreams...or fantasies. For once the bedtime routine didn't bother her. Because tomorrow or the next day, sometime soon, she would see Lucas again. Not just see him.

She pressed her fingertips to her mouth, revelling in the tenderness of the still swollen flesh. It didn't make sense that he wanted her broken body. There must be an element of pity, perhaps of nostalgia in his desire. Whatever his motives, she wasn't so full of pride that she would reject the opportunity of one more chance of making love with Lucas. Sex. It would be sex. She mustn't forget.

"Your father tells me that Hall boy is hanging around again."

"Hardly a boy, Mum. He's nearly thirty." Harriet carefully kept her voice level. She'd know this was coming ever since the other night. A sigh from her father only added to her annoyance. "And I wouldn't say hanging around. We met at work and he came to dinner. Once."

"Is that so? Thirty? I suppose he's married by now."

"He doesn't wear a ring." Harriet had wondered about that. He kept fiddling with his fingers but the skin at first glance seemed uniformly tanned.

"Probably a de-facto relationship in that case. Although some men don't like to wear a ring. He might be one of those."

"One of those...what? You're the one always preaching about giving people the benefit of the doubt."

Her mother's thin face flushed. "It's easy to see he isn't the type to hang around when trouble comes."

"Don't be such a revisionist. I sent him away remember. You thought it was the right thing to do at the time. You told me it was the right thing to do."

"He never would have married you. It was all for the best in the long run."

"You don't know that. His sister and brother are both married. Maybe it runs in the family."

Flustered, Caro concentrated on serving up the chicken casserole. "Is that enough for you?"

"More than enough. It's not like I have to run marathons."

Seating herself at the table, her mother pursed her lips, glancing sideways at her husband. "You shouldn't have given up the ballroom dancing. You were so good at it. Basketball isn't quite the same thing."

"It took up too much time. While I was a university it wasn't a problem, but now I'm working I can't commit to three nights a week and most weekends. Not to mention the travel for the competitions." She poked at her chicken leg.

"Besides, I still help out with the beginner classes. Enough to keep my hand in."

"You know you don't have to work."

"I do. We've gone through this before. Tell her Dad. I'm not going to use my legs as an excuse to become a sponge."

"Leave it, Caro. The girl needs to use her brain."

Harriet smiled gratefully at her father. At least he understood that much. Even if he was too anxious about his wife to argue with her. Harriet couldn't remember a time when Caro hadn't been frail and nervy. Not that she hadn't a good reason. Things hadn't been easy for her for so many years. If only she could get over the whole protective thing. It was almost an obsession. She wouldn't leave it of course. Her next words proved it.

"Very well. All the same I hope you aren't encouraging Lucas Hall to hang around. He was a bad influence the first time. Distracting you. Men like him only want one thing."

Seething, Harriet pushed her plate away. "If Lucas wants sex I'll be glad to give it to him. God knows it's been long enough. There are worse things people can do. He at least made me feel good about myself."

The clatter of her mother's cutlery on the glass top table jarred. "Harriet Emerson. This isn't like you. I can see his influence already. Until he came along your behaviour was always exemplary. Speak to your daughter, Jack."

Spinning away from the table, she shook her head. "Don't bother. I'm going home. I'll be back when you remember I'm an adult. I make my own decisions. I choose my own friends. If I want to have sex, I'll do that too. I may be a cripple but I'm a woman, not a child."

"Well don't come crying to us when he loves you and leaves you. Do you really think someone like him would hang around for the day to day grind like we do? Take you to hospitals, help you when your knees play up. If it weren't for him, you wouldn't have had the accident in the first place."

"It wasn't his fault. Even the police reports said it wasn't his fault."

"He's no good for you, Harriet. He won't be there for you when you need him."

"At least he wouldn't want to harvest my organs. He might break my heart, but I'd get to keep the pieces."

The sudden silence that greeted her angry words settled over her, dark and heavy. Slowly she turned the wheelchair to face her parents. Guilt sucked the air from her lungs at her mother's white face. "I'm sorry. That was a low blow."

Jack sighed. "We shouldn't have pushed you about Lucas." His arm was around her mother's shoulders. The guilt clawed at her again, knowing the grey in her mother's soft brown hair, the white in her father's, owed something to her own actions.

"I thought you liked him. You always welcomed him when he came around."

"We did, your mother is just worried. We know how hurt you were last time when he left."

"I don't blame him for that and you shouldn't either. He wouldn't have gone if I hadn't lied to him. He's really not that kind of person. In fact, the whole reason he came back to Australia was to look after his mother. Surely that proves he has some sense of responsibility."

"You know Lucas and I spoke after we met at your apartment?"

"I supposed you would." She'd been wondering whether there'd been some kind of confrontation. Especially as Lucas hadn't called since.

"He was shocked at your injuries. You must have been very convincing."

"You paid for the drama classes. They had to be good for something."

"All the same. I'm still a little surprised he left so abruptly and didn't come back. He was only supposed to be gone a year. He seemed keen at the time. A fact he confirmed the other night."

"He didn't want to go without me. He told me he would relinquish the scholarship. I had to be really awful to him to convince him I wasn't worth it."

Her parents shared a glance, her father's voice gruff. "We didn't realise you were thinking of going to the U.S. with him. When were we going to find out?"

Biting her lip Harriet shrugged. "It doesn't matter now. The point is, he's unlikely to want any relationship with me, even if he could adjust to my disability."

"Why not? He'd be very lucky to have you." Her mother was funny... and illogical. Up in arms because a boy she disapproved of and a relationship she'd been arguing against only minutes ago might be unwanted by the boy in question.

"I said some things no man could forgive. I made fun of him. Lots of things. Horrible things."

Her father shook his head. "That was wrong of you. Very wrong. You'll have to apologise."

"I did. But I don't know if he believes me."

"Maybe you'll get the chance to prove it to him."

Harriet stared back at her father. "I'd like that. I'd like us to be friends again. Even if nothing else."

Reaching out, he stroked her hair lightly. "You do the right thing and something good will come of it."

~

As the ball left her fingers, Harriet rocked with the impact from another chair. Grabbing the wheels, she spun away, with a last glance to check the ball went through the hoop. The cheer from her teammates confirmed the score just as the buzzer went for full time. They'd won, but only just. She'd missed an easy goal early in the game.

It wasn't precisely because of Lucas being in the stands. It was the unexpectedness of it. After not coming near her for almost two weeks, she'd resigned herself to not seeing him. So halfway through the first half when she spotted Jimmie and beside him Lucas, she'd fumbled the ball as she sent it towards the target.

Luckily the other girls in the team were on it instantly and they retrieved the situation. Stealing another look at Lucas, a surge of anger burned low in her belly. He couldn't do this. Just waltz in and out of her life as he pleased. Throughout the men's game she stuck close to her teammates, careful not to look in his direction. When she did look, at the end of the game, he was gone.

"That was close." Jimmie's voice brought her from her reverie. The tall figure behind him looked down at her unsmiling.

"Hello, Harry. An exciting game."

With a shrug, she edged away. "Nerve wracking is more like it. I thought we were bound to lose."

"I saw you miss the first shot. Did you get distracted?"

He knew, dammit. "Probably. If you'll excuse me, I need to get someone to take my other chair down to the car."

"I've got it." Jimmy stood with the sporting wheelchair, a beaming smile on his face. He immediately turned away, steering between the diminishing crowd.

"He's a nice young lad."

Harriet looked up at Lucas, resenting his easy

assumption of intimacy. "He is. Considering his background, he's amazing."

"Not good?"

"Foster care and a lot of moving around."

"I knew that. He told me when I took him home after the last game. What happened to his family?"

"No father and the mother relinquished him to the state when he was six. I'm not breaking confidentiality with this. It's common knowledge. He doesn't know how to keep secrets."

"A nice characteristic."

They'd reached the car and Jimmie quickly hopped out of the wheelchair. "It's okay Jimmie. I don't mind you having a ride."

With a sheepish grin, he took the keys and Lucas helped him load the chair into the car. "It's fun. For me I mean." He flushed with embarrassment and jogged off to the only other car in the isolated car park. A black Lamborghini. Harriet looked at Lucas with a wry expression.

He nodded. "Yes. I still like big black beasts with powerful motors."

"Do you still ride?"

"No. Motorbikes lost their charm for me a long time ago."

"Well, I guess that thing would be just as much of a chick magnet as the Ducati was."

"You think so?" His emerald eyes glinted wickedly. "Does that mean you'll come on a date with me?"

"No but thank you anyway." She moved away to open the door of the Focus.

"What's with the chill factor, Harry? I thought we'd reached an understanding. To be friends at least."

His long fingers ploughed his hair, leaving it standing up

in ragged spikes. For the first time she looked at him closely. "You look tired."

"I just flew in from Sydney. That's why we were late for the game."

"You've been in Sydney all this time?" The anger dropped to a low simmer. All the same, he could have told her, rather than leaving her wondering.

"Hell, no. That would have been easier. I've done the rounds, Washington, New York, London and Dubai. But you know that."

"How would I know? I haven't seen you for weeks."

"I left a message." His eyes shifted to look over at the Lamborghini.

"You left it with Jimmie? He's not good with verbal messages."

"So, you thought...Damn. I knew I should have made sure I spoke to you, but you were in a meeting and I had to leave. The U.S. military waits for no man."

"Are you trying to impress me? Because it's working."

He rubbed his hands together with a sly chuckle. "Soooo. About that date?"

Her father's words about doing the right thing nudged her. It would be an opportunity to apologise properly. "All right. Where abouts?"

"I thought a restaurant."

"Is it accessible? For a wheelchair I mean."

"Of course. I do my research."

"And when?"

"Tomorrow. I was hoping to come for another swim, but I'll be a fraction late. Meetings until at least five."

Lucas in his swimsuit was not to be missed. "I have a spare card, so I wouldn't have to buzz you in. You could meet me at the pool."

Harriet was in the pool when he arrived, the dark reddish bikini contrasting with the paleness of her body, lit by the underwater lighting. The rest of the pavilion remained dim apart from the half a dozen circles illuminated by the overhead lights. She swam strongly with her arms but from this angle he saw how her legs dragged below the knee joints.

He could see Jack's point about amputation maybe being the better option. His expressed opinion that eventually she may have to consider it if her condition worsened had haunted his dreams ever since. At this moment he was glad she hadn't lost her legs. Even if she would never dance for him the way she'd done in those months together.

He'd never understood the meaning of the word grace, until he'd met Harriet. The way she moved, smooth and elegant, he'd could have watched her forever. Even a simple thing like walking up the stairs had him mesmerised. Because she never really walked anywhere. Not in the way he understood walking. Putting one foot after another. She skipped, she waltzed, she dazzled. She been so alive, not like new Harriet with the fixed smile, awkward painful gait and calloused palms from the wheels of her chair.

Dumping his towel beside hers, he dived into the water, careful to keep to the side away from Harriet's trajectory. He had a feeling she paused but when he emerged and glanced back, she still moved up the pool steadily. Disappointed, he kept swimming, until he felt the water change as she halted up near the stairs. He joined her, drifting the last few meters until he touched the tiled surface.

Propping himself on the edge of the pool on his elbow, he watched her twist her long hair to remove the water. The water trickled down her chest to gather in her shallow cleavage. He swallowed with a noisy gulp and dragged his gaze up to her face. "Are you finished?"

"I'm not sure. I lost count somewhere along the way."

He pushed away from the side and floated to where Harriet was standing, her weight supported by the water that came to just below her breasts. "How come you don't use flippers?"

Harriet edged away slightly. "I do, but only a couple of times a week."

He let his legs brush against hers as he dropped them to the bottom of the pool to bring himself to a standing position directly in front of her. "You haven't grown much in seven years. It's hard to tell in your chair."

She smiled ruefully. "I believe I'm actually a couple of centimetres shorter, truth be told."

Lucas looked down at the delicate face tilted to look up at him as he towered over her, almost but not quite touching. "I'll have to test that out."

She licked her lips nervously, her eyes on his mouth. "How are you going to do that?"

"Easy, by doing something I used to do when I knew you before." He sank down in the water, his knees barely touching the outside of her calves before coming to rest against her knee braces. "Is that okay?"

"It's fine. The braces stop them flexing too much." Her words came out breathless and husky. She was just as affected as he was, her eyes darkening to purple as her pupils dilated. He was still trying to adjust to the new and volatile emotions that surfaced under the impact of learning the truth about what happened after the accident. That raw sexual need tempered by the urge to guard her, protect her.

The anxiety that tightened his chest when he thought about her pain then and now.

Here, in the water, they were equals again, not separated by the metal framework of the wheelchair, by his height compared to her stature. *It would be the same in bed.* The thought burned through his body, sparking electrical impulses that pumped adrenaline and blood to his extremities, feeding the ache in his gut.

Her breathing quickened as his hands wrapped around her waist, his thumb stroking down to rest on her navel. She was so slender, almost boyish with square shoulders from the swimming and her small breasts. With one hand he reached up to undo the ties of her bikini top while the other cupped her behind, bring her hips into alignment with his. "Lucas..."

"It's okay. We'll hear the lift bell if anyone comes."

He began at the sensitive point on her neck just below her ear, teeth and tongue tasting her chlorine tainted flesh while his hand rested gently on her shoulder, thumb drawing circles on the silken skin over her collarbone. Pulling away, he stared at her breasts, cupping one of them with his hand. He remembered the nipple as more of a pale pink, the tip slightly puffy and the nipple itself small, blending into the surrounding flesh. Now they were darker, the raspberry coloured nipple prominent and becoming more so as his fingers kneaded the smooth silky skin.

Dipping his head, he took the hard bead into his mouth, his groin tightening as his dick throbbed against her thigh. She gave a little moan and he thought for a minute he might explode there and then. It was no good. He couldn't keep things under control.

Harriet whimpered as he released her nipple and he

licked it apologetically before retying her top. "Sorry baby. I think we need to take this somewhere more private."

He scooped her up and carried her to her chair, helping her dry herself before she sat. She said nothing, wide eyed and chewing her bottom lip as he pulled his tee over his head. If anything, she looked more nervous than he felt.

As the lift dropped down to her floor, his own stomach dropped at her distant expression.

She frowned suddenly. "Where are your clothes?"

"I dropped them in your apartment before I came up to the pool."

"Oh...that was sensible."

"Harriet..." She gave a hard push on the wheel as she entered the apartment and spun to face him. He closed the door and stood waiting.

"Lucas."

"Harry, if I'm going too fast we can slow down." It would kill him, but he didn't want to stuff this up.

She blushed, a paler shade to her bikini. "I was wondering. Would you like to help me out in the shower? It might be quicker..."

*Or not.* He held the towels in front of his body as another rush of heat surged from the pit of his stomach to his chest and back again. "Sure thing." *Crap.* He sounded like a mouse on steroids.

Harriet eyed Lucas warily. He looked like he was ready to jump her one minute and the next he withdrew. He'd seemed out of control in the pool but suddenly he backed off. This hot and cold Lucas was hard to gauge. His arousal pressed against her told one story, but his stiff demeanour in the lift made her nervous. What if he was having second thoughts? She wasn't even sure how this would work.

"Well? Are we having this shower?"

*We?* Him, her, together. She didn't dare look down, sure her nipples were sticking out like guns on a fembot. He'd brought her to aching excitement only to pull away. After seven years of sterile nothingness, her body was out of control, wet and wanting.

"If you like." How inane was that. She hoped he more than liked or this was going to be humiliation central.

Without looking behind, she went down the hallway, into her bedroom. She paused until he caught up and entered the bathroom. He'd followed her this far. That had to be good.

"What can I do?" He stood, leaning against the doorframe with the towels held against his stomach. His eyes scanned the white tiled room, lingering on the stainless-steel rails in the shower and then shifted to look at the ones around the toilet. "This is a pretty good setup."

"We bought if off the plan, so it was done especially." She moved over to the shower, wondering what he must be thinking. The room screamed disability. Emphasised her inadequacies. *This is a mistake.*

"It isn't." She jerked around to look at him. "It's not a mistake, Harriet."

She'd spoken aloud? Talking to herself? Next, she'd be adding mentally unstable to her CV. "It's not exactly sexy."

"You are." He dropped the towels on the hamper and came closer, squatting down, balancing with one hand on her chair. "Harry. If you aren't comfortable, I'll leave you alone." His hand stroked her thigh above the brace, his fingertips almost brushing the fabric of her bikini. "But I would love to stay."

Prickles under her skin burned their way to the surface under his touch. A gush of moisture anticipated his possession. "Ahuh...All right. If you just leave me alone for a minute. Then I'll be ready."

She rushed to do what was necessary before he returned, seating herself on the fold down bench in the shower as his knock came on the door.

Bunching the towel around her, she drew a calming breath. "I'm ready." He was ready too if the rigid shape in his swimmers could be believed. "Is that a sonic screwdriver in your pocket...?"

His chuckle at the familiar quip warmed her as his thumbs dug under the waistband and released his erection.

"I guess you could say that. On the other hand, I'm very pleased to see you."

He dropped the togs onto the hamper with the towels and joined her in the large shower area, his skin pale gold apart from the narrow untanned strip across his pelvis. No shyness there, but he didn't need to be shy with that kind of endowment. Her mouth was suddenly dry as he stopped in front of her, his penis right in her line of sight, upright against his stomach in its nest of black curls.

"What's with the towel, Harry? Are you cold?"

"Just a little nervous. It's been a long time for me." She tilted her chin up, forcing herself to look at his face.

"It's..." His lips compressed over the words and she wondered what he would have revealed. She didn't want to know, did she?

Long fingers pried her hands away from their clutch on the towel. "Trust me, Harry."

Trust. Lucas knew instinctively that was the big question. He'd lost her trust by walking when she'd pushed him away. She thought all she was offering now was sex, all he was wanting. He wanted a whole lot more. But it was a start and here was as good a place as any. They'd done so little before, been so cautious.

She'd been a good girl even back then, focused on her studies, her free time filled with dance classes and drama lessons. No time for a boyfriend. Her parents sent her to a religious school and for Harriet it meant something. For him, newly discovering the joys of a girlfriend after years of awkward interactions with the female of the species, the unwelcome restrictions had been less about some old-fashioned ideal of purity and more about keeping Harriet.

He'd known she would walk away if he made it about sex. She'd clung to the ideals her parents instilled in her. Nice folks, good people, but over-protective.

The towel came free and he hung it over one of the rails. "I like this bench. I can get closer."

Her hand came up immediately, the slender fingers wrapping around his swollen shaft. It felt so bloody good. "How close do you want to be?"

God, he loved it when she smiled like that, wicked yet still sweet. There were no surprises with her body. He'd been afraid there might be hidden scars apart from those on her legs. A little bit skinny, her ribs showing under the pert breasts and her pelvic bones visible low on her stomach. The neat triangle of golden hair matched the darker brows and lashes rather than the silvery blonde of her hair. He glimpsed the shadowy depths at the apex of her slightly parted thighs and everything tightened down below.

She gripped him harder as he twitched, tugging him closer, bringing one leg between her knees and the other jammed against the bench. He watched, captivated as she licked her lips. "All right?"

He nodded, sucking in air as she pulled the foreskin back and licked the sensitive exposed tip. He wanted to watch but the pleasure as she licked the underside from his balls to his knob was too much. He steadied himself, winding his fingers through her hair as her other hand explored his sack, squeezing and pressing one finger on the receptive spot just behind. How the hell did she know so much? She took him into her mouth, the warmth moist cavern swallowing his dick down to where her hand wrapped around his shaft. He wasn't going to last. Too much anticipation, too much need.

Opening his eyes, he sought out Harriet's gaze. "I have to pull out." Her eyes widened as she made a small negative movement of her head. Her knuckle pressed hard into his prostate and it was too late. His tangled fingers jerked in her hair as she swallowed him deep, taking him beyond control, beyond thinking as he fell into pleasure, his knees giving way, falling heavily onto the hard edge of the bench. The pain spiked him into awareness and he braced himself against the shower wall, taking deep breaths.

Harriet's touch on his abs, delicate and warm brought him back. He dropped to his knees, searching her face. "I'm sorry."

Her hand trailed across his left shoulder, fingertips tracing the almost invisible scars. "Was it so bad?"

The rueful quirk of her lips along with the warmth of her gaze made a nonsense of his anxiety. "You know it was pretty damn good for me."

A delicate flush pinked her cheekbones. "I'm glad." Her fingers still hesitated over his shoulder, the roughness of the skin the only obvious reminder of the gravel rash that left his shoulder bloody and raw after the accident. That and the broken arm had been quick to mend. Unlike Harriet's wounds.

"You show me yours and I'll show you mine." He whispered against her ear and saw the pulse at the base of her throat flutter.

"You don't really want to see them." He moved his lips to the hollow at the base of her throat letting his tongue dip into the shadowed skin. "I want to find out all the things that have changed in the last seven years since I last knew you."

He ran a hand over her bare skin. "But first we better shower and get you warm."

"I need to get out of my braces. It would be quicker if you helped."

"Your wish is my command"

She giggled as he bowed, his nudity and kneeling posture an odd contrast with the old-fashioned gesture. Memories of other times, other occasions when he'd made her laugh sobered her, but he wasn't looking at her face.

He was studying the braces on her knees with interest, his long fingers probing and prodding until he finally started to pull the Velcro straps to release them. "Is there anything I should watch out for?"

Harriet nodded. "Try not to twist the knee."

Carefully supporting each leg, Lucas removed the moulded braces and put them aside.

"What would happen if they twisted?"

"They could pop out of alignment or the ligaments could get stretched."

He was adjusting the water temperature as he spoke,

lifting the shower hose from the wall mount. "Is it painful when it happens?"

"A bit. But it's very rare if I'm cautious. It's why I have to strap them to the chair to play basketball."

His fingers in her hair, lifting the long strands to make sure the warm water flowed through the thick layers, soothed her. She didn't protest as he shampooed and rinsed but when he began to soap her body she wiggled uncomfortably.

"I'm not a baby. I can help you know."

He planted a kiss on her nose. "And spoil my fun?"

All the same, he let her wash herself, using the fixed shower rose on the other wall to bathe himself, distracting her with the sight of his body all slick with soapy water.

He dried her legs for her paying particular attention to her toes. "Here's my favourite." He tweaked the knobbly middle toe she'd broken in a fall at ballet rehearsal. He'd said he liked that she had something imperfect, otherwise he really would believe she was a Faerie escaped from the Elven lands. There was a lot more imperfection now.

He seated her on the edge of the bed, a towel swathed turban like around her wet hair. For a moment her body rebelled at losing the touch of his bare skin against hers as he unwrapped her head. When he began to towel her hair, it was a simple matter to slip her arms around his waist and steady herself by resting against his chest. As she lay her cheek against the steady beat of his heart a calmness seeped into her. It had been so long since she'd felt this way. Tingling alive right down to her fingertips yet harbouring a deep contentment.

It was the sex. It had to be. It couldn't be more than physical. She wouldn't let it be more. Friends with benefits he'd said and that suited her fine. Love was too painful. She had no intention of going that route again. All she wanted was to assuage this physical ache that had reignited when Lucas had come back into her life and presumably the same thing was driving him.

"This bed is higher than average. Is that deliberate?"

Harriet had to concentrate on his words as she lost focus, inhaling the warm scent of his body. Melting her like chocolate under the summer sun.

She stirred herself, lifting her head away from its smooth, velvet skinned pillow. "Yes. I find low beds hard to get out of."

There was a low rumble of laugher that echoed through her chest. "That's not such a bad thing, is it? But I can think of other things useful about high beds." He pressed his thighs against her stomach and the visual images his words invoked brought out goose bumps on her skin. He finished her hair and his fingers combed out the tangles, running lightly over her scalp and down her back. *Did every touch from this man have electrical impulses?* Closing her eyes, she savoured the sensation of skin warming under the slight pressure of his fingertips.

"Now for the braces." Lucas scooped her legs up and turned her so she was lying on the bed, her damp hair spread out over the pillow. "Are these the ones you need now?"

Harriet opened her eyes and nodded as she saw the padded braces in his hands. "I can do it."

He grinned as he held the braces out of her reach, lying them beside her on the bed. "You let me do it this time. The scientific mind wants to know how it works." Taking his weight on one arm, he leaned over, bracing himself across her legs. A crease formed between his brows as he studied her knees, examining the multiple scars, running his fingers along each one.

Harriet expected to feel self-conscious or embarrassed but the expression on his face was the same one he used to wear when working out a complex computer problem and somehow that made it easier. She couldn't have borne sympathy or horror from Lucas.

"This one is different. What happened here?" His fingers were running along a silvery scar that began at the back of her right knee and up the inside of her thigh almost to the groin. "Isn't it unusual to do such a long incision these days."

Harriet was trying desperately to control the quiver as his fingers rested at the top of the scar and he saw her face and moved his hand away.

"Sorry. Did I hurt you?"

She looked at him unbelievingly. Only moments ago, he'd been flirting but now he had obviously been totally side-tracked by his interest in her injuries.

"It was an emergency. An aneurism in the artery burst and they had trouble locating it. There wasn't enough time for a scan."

Something in her voice must have caught his attention and he looked up at her face. She tried to look nonchalant but couldn't hide the flush in her skin and the arousal in her eyes.

"I'm sorry, Harry, was I neglecting you?"

With a half-smile he climbed onto the bed to kneel astride her right leg. Ducking down, he ran the tip of his tongue up the line of the scar. A tingle shot through her body, bouncing around like a ball in an old arcade game, pinging her breasts and sending a rush of heat to the pit of her stomach.

He pulled away, smiling at her murmur of protest. "Just

in case I get distracted later." Propping herself on her elbows, she watched as he strapped on her braces. Smoothing the Velcro tabs into place. "All good?"

"All good."

His mouth returned immediately to the task of tasting the skin of her inner thigh. *Very good.* That was something she'd always appreciated about Lucas. His consideration as a lover even in the short time they were together. The first time they'd gone all the way hadn't been that great. There'd been more pain than she expected. Afterwards he'd been so tender, so apologetic. But he made it up to her. So much so, she hadn't wanted to leave, to go home.

"Are you with me, Harry?"

He must had felt her tense at the memories and she forced herself to relax as he parted her legs with careful hands. Cool air flooded her heated flesh as his fingers smoothed her inner thighs. Internal muscles clenched, intensifying the ache.

"With bells on."

"Legs okay?"

Flexing the knees slightly she nodded. "Quite all right."

His chuckle reassured, even as the glow in his emerald eyes triggered goose-bumps. "Time to get down to business."

7

---

Kneeling upright between her legs, he looked a magnificent beast, clean, tanned flesh over sculpted muscle, his erection straining upwards towards his navel, framed by dark curling hair. *And she'd been worried about his recovery time?* Reaching up, she ran her fingertip down the prominent vein, laughing when he twitched.

"Tease." But he was smiling as he said it. He dropped forward, propping his upper body on his arms. The hairs on his forearms tickled the taut flesh of her ribcage and she squirmed.

His lips traced her jaw and she squirmed again as his moist tongue delved into her ear. "Now who's the tease?"

He nipped her lobe in retaliation and slowly rubbed his chest over her peaking breasts. "That would be me."

Growling, she linked her hands behind his head, trying to pull him down for a kiss but he laughed, resisting her. This time he lowered his hips and his erection pressed against her belly briefly. Too briefly. She tried to lift her hips, but her knees wouldn't co-operate. She gasped at the sharp pain and growled again with annoyance.

Lucas stiffened immediately, sitting back on his heels. "What happened?"

Evading his eyes, she muttered, "Nothing."

"Don't lie to me, Harriet."

The firm tone brought her gaze back to his face. His lowered brows and tight mouth warned her not to prevaricate. He was right. There'd been too many lies between them. She forced back tears of frustration. "If you must know, my knee hurt. I hope you like making love to a dead body, because I'm about as useless as corpse."

His mouth twisted into a smirk. "Necrophilia isn't my thing, but for you...maybe."

"Ewww. That's gross."

His long fingers brushed her wet lashes. "Harry, you have to be honest. Especially about your legs. I don't want to hurt you."

But he would. Only it wouldn't be her legs but her heart. Sooner or later, probably sooner, he'd leave again. "I'm sorry. It's so frustrating just lying here."

"You mean I have you at my mercy?"

She didn't want to smile, but his broad grin and the wicked sparkle in his eyes made it hard to resist.

"That's better." He kissed her lips, turning her half-hearted effort into a full-blown smile.

He kissed her again, properly, his firm mouth softening as he sucked her bottom lip. Tentatively she tasted him. He took her tongue into his mouth, hot and wet as his teeth scraped the surface and tugged again at her lip, drawing them both up and releasing them. His hard length pushed against her mound as he deepened the kiss, sealing her mouth, grinding against her with teeth and the strength of his thighs.

The most she could do was tilt her pelvis seeking more

and lower, the trickle of moisture between her legs increasing with the throbbing ache of arousal. She whimpered into his mouth and the whimper became a moan.

Lucas pulled away with a soft snicker. "For someone claiming to be a corpse, you sure do pack a punch." His hand slid down her body to grasp the base of his shaft. Squeezing it tightly, his knuckles so very close to her clit she writhed at the sensation.

"Please. You. Are. Killing. Me."

He straightened, and she groaned. "Get back here, Lucas Hall." She reached to put her hands on his shoulders, but he laughingly pulled away.

"No, this is my turn to explore. Be patient."

Gritting her teeth, she glared up at him. "Patience be damned."

"Swearing, Harriet? I'm shocked." He tucked a strand of hair behind her ear. "I'll make it good for you. I can swear to that."

His thumb across her lips tantalised and she opened her mouth, sinking her teeth into the pad.

"Naughty. I'll have to punish you for that."

His head came closer and she held her breath, waiting. As his teeth sank into her nipple, the sharp pain echoed a spasm in her groin and her breath came out in a huff. He soothed it with his tongue and repeated the process on her other breast, back and forth until she grabbed his hair, tugging at it to pull him away. "It's too much."

Cupping her breasts with his hands, he nodded, dropping a kiss between them. The next kiss, open mouthed, moist and warm landed on her navel. The kisses crept lower, leaving damp patches on her skin that cooled as they dried, her stomach tightening at the unfamiliar sensation.

His breath fanned the light covering of hair on her mound and lower, the warm air cooling the damp flesh. He mouthed the nerve centre and his teeth pinched it lightly at the same time as he squeezed her breasts, thumb and forefinger compressing her nipples. The thrumming pulse between her legs exploded.

In the midst of her pleasure, she remained aware of Lucas, his mouth prolonging her pleasure, his hands kneading the sensitive peaks of her breasts. Another wave came a then another, taking her higher until blackness overwhelmed her, a scented darkness holding a secret she reached out for, an urgency in the action that stayed with her in the slow descent to reality, to Lucas, his head resting on her belly, his hands soft over her breasts.

Lifting his head, Lucas met Harriet's gaze. Stripped bare in the immediate aftermath, he could see the vulnerability and a touch of confusion. *She hadn't expected that?* An odd reaction considering their past. They'd learned what little they'd known of the art of love together, their bodies so attuned it took no more than a look or a touch to set them humming. Had that broken trust intruded into even the physical side of the relationship?

He moved to lie beside her, his hand stroking her breast and teasing her nipple. "Okay, Harry?"

"Very okay, Lucas." She sighed, and it didn't sound like a happy sigh. "But I want more." Her hand traced the planes of his abdomen to the trail of hair below his navel. The back of her hand brushed against his erection. "I want all of you, Lucas."

He captured her hand before she could grab hold and linked their fingers, bringing them to his lips, nibbling at the knuckles. "I didn't intend this to happen, Harry. I thought we'd be going out to dinner to get to know each other again. Not…"

"Getting to know each other like this?"

"I need the answer to a question before we take this any further."

Harriet struggled onto her side to face him. Lucas steadied her with his free hand on her shoulder. They lay facing each other with linked hands between them. There was something intimate about it that hadn't been there when they were making love.

"I need to know about the day in the hospital." His voice came out strained and he pushed on, watching her intently. "I know you lied about your recovery. How much truth was there in the rest of what you said that day?"

Gold tipped lashes fluttered as her lids lowered, trying to conceal her thoughts. "Only as much as was necessary to make you believe it."

His fingers tightened convulsively on her shoulder and she opened her eyes wide. He eased his grip, afraid of bruising the delicate skin. "Why, Harriet? Why did you have to be so cruel? What did you gain from breaking my heart?"

Her hand wavered against his chest "Hearts don't break, Lucas. Yours is still beating. And you got your freedom."

"What if I didn't want it, Harry?"

"I wanted you to have it. I knew you wouldn't go if you had the choice. I had to kill the dream."

The anger simmering at the pit of his stomach bubbled into life again. "Well you succeeded in that. Stone dead. And your parents, what part did they play in this? They knew what you planned to do, didn't they?"

Harriet squirmed a little under his regard. "We talked about it. They were in it for the long haul whatever. It seemed a waste to drag you into the pit as well. You were only just starting your career."

"So, you cut me loose just like that. I loved you, Harry. I wanted to spend my life with you. For better or worse."

"Past tense. In any case, it would have been all worse."

He examined her sorrowful face, the droop of her lips, still bruised from his kisses. "I suppose so. You didn't think much of my staying power, did you?"

"It wasn't that. You deserved your chance. If you stayed with me, you wouldn't be where you are today."

She had no idea about his staying power or anything else. He could understand her point of view. Her reasons behind her actions. Even admire her for it. But the way she did it stuck in his craw. There was no respect in telling someone you weren't good enough, that you were ashamed to be seen with them. That his stumbling social skills would be a disadvantage for her brilliant career.

How many slurs were lies to create the effect she wanted? The brilliant career never eventuated and apparently, she'd known that when she threw those insults at him. Yes, there had been an element of truth in what she said. He had been hopeless in public in those days. But until that day, she'd never indicated a problem with it.

"Lucas? Are you all right?"

He released her shoulder and ran his finger along her chin and down her throat. It was true, he hadn't planned on getting this far tonight, but with Harriet so responsive, so needy...Why not? He needed it. More than she could know.

She didn't protest as he put her arms above her head, wrapping her fingers around the timber rail.

"Lucas?"

He pressed his dick against her stomach and she sucked in a breath. Needy. She wanted this. As much as he did, if not more.

"Just don't say anything, Harry."

The sweet taste of her as he lapped at her throat; her soft mouth, tremulous under his. God, he'd missed this. Missed her. The adrenaline buzz of making millions, the satisfaction of a well scripted program didn't compare to this. His hands roamed ceaselessly, the silken skin smooth under his fingers, her breasts soft yet firm. He rubbed himself against her slick folds, her moans heady and arousing. She was wet with desire, still swollen from before. He was more than ready, a heavy ache in his balls despite his earlier release.

Suckling her breasts, he slid down to re-position her legs so his body fitted between them without straining her knees. Her writhing body chafed his nipples into points as he moved over it to possess her mouth again, moist and hot and sweet as honey. With one hand he positioned himself. "I don't have condoms."

Her breath puffed against his cheek as she lay suddenly still under him. "I'm clean."

"I was thinking of pregnancy."

There was a long moment as she looked up at him with something dark in her eyes. It stirred something in his throat, his heart, as he wondered what their children would have been like. Harriet, the only child, had wanted a big family. He'd been more cautious. Now it wouldn't happen and irrationally he wanted it. She licked her lips, speaking with an effort.

"It's the wrong time."

She remained still, and he took a moment to realise what she waited for. "I'm clean too. I haven't been with anyone recently." He could have told her the truth. But he wasn't about to expose himself at this point.

Her sceptical look annoyed him, but he swallowed it down, deliberately rubbing himself against her. She had no reason to trust him. Not when he was holding things back. "We can wait until we have condoms if you want."

Harriet groaned, tilting her hips to try and capture him. Lucas held her gaze and she nodded. At her capitulation he pushed into her. She was so tight he looked down at her anxiously. Her lids closed with a flutter of lashes and his gut tightened. The slow curl of her mouth reassured, and he could breathe again. With a shudder he began a slow movement that deepened his stroke each time.

As he buried himself to the hilt, she was with him. Dark blue, almost violet eyes locked with his as the pace increased. Conscious of her legs he tried to keep it smooth, but it was hard to keep control. Harriet came first, convulsing around him with a gasping scream. It tipped him over the edge, heart fast and breathing heavy as his orgasm smashed into him and rolled through his body.

*Empty.* Maybe he could understand her confusion. It shouldn't be so good, so primal, with all that lay between them. The anger, the resentment, the grief for things lost.

Lucas rested limply against her, his chest heaving as much with emotion as physical release. When her arms crept around his waist, he fought off the wave of emotion, taking a deep breath. Carefully he disengaged, rolling to the side and taking her with him. "I must be heavy."

Snuggling into him she demurred. "I like it. It feels real. I feel real."

His fingers traced her brow and over her ears. "You've always been real, my faerie girl."

Harriet stiffened, pulling away. "Don't say that. She's gone, Lucas. There's no such creature anymore."

With a hold on her upper arm, he dragged her onto his chest and kissed her. "Have it your way." He kept her close against his chest until he felt her soften against him. "You'll always be a faerie girl to me." There was no response to his soft murmur. She was asleep.

"I owe you dinner."

Harriet stirred into wakefulness. Warm arms held her, and her head rested in the curve of a male shoulder. However long she'd slept, she felt amazing. A little tender in places but so good in others.

"We've missed our reservation."

Focusing on Lucas with difficulty she lifted her head. "Will they be mad?"

"I doubt it. They probably gave our table to someone else when we didn't turn up."

"Do you want something to eat?" She didn't feel particularly hungry at the moment, but she wasn't properly awake either.

"A bit hungry. Is there anything in the fridge we could have?"

"Sandwich fixings. That would be quickest."

He rolled away, leaving her chilled and a little confused. The warm, tender lover was gone, and the hard, practical man was back. "I'll go grab my things from the other bedroom."

Her chair still sat over by the bathroom door where

Lucas left it earlier. With a mild curse she hung over the edge of the bed, groping for the crutches. Halfway to the bathroom, Lucas returned, a pair of jeans covering his long legs. "You should have yelled."

"It's all right. I'm all sticky anyway, so I would have mucked up the chair." Standing awkwardly, she wished Lucas would stop staring. With him decently covered, her own nudity seemed prurient. "Why don't you go find the sandwich stuff while I clean up?"

His mouth opened and closed and he nodded, leaving her to it. He probably meant to offer to help and thought better of it. By the time she cleaned up, all she wanted to do was go back to bed. Quickly she pulled a baggy t-shirt over her head and wheeled herself to the kitchen.

A stack of sandwiches waited on the bench along with a jug of apple juice. Lucas had his head in the fridge replacing the butter and other bits and pieces. They'd barely made themselves comfortable when the phone rang. Glancing at the clock, Harriet murmured a disbelieving protest. "It can't be."

"Hi.... Yes, Lucas is here.... just swimming.... we've been chatting about old times......sure I'll ask him." She put her hand over the mouthpiece "Mum wants to know if you'd like to join us for my birthday dinner, Sunday evening. Don't feel obliged. You know how she is."

Lucas nodded. "Tell her I'd like to come."

"Really? Are you sure?"

"I'm sure."

"Yes Mum, he said he would.... wine.... I'll check"

Lucas nodded again. "He says okay.... all right, thanks. See you then."

"And they ring you every night without fail?" Lucas enquired, picking up another sandwich.

"Not usually on Thursday nights because I'm never home before nine. If they know I'm going to be out somewhere they might not ring but it's generally prearranged. That doesn't happen often."

Lucas rubbed his bare toes against her foot. "And this has been going on since you left home nearly two years ago? What happens if you get a steady boyfriend or...something permanent?"

"In that unlikely event, I think they'll assume he's looking after me. I've been trying to convince them I can look after myself for years with no success. I don't expect things to change in a hurry."

"You really aren't looking for another permanent relationship?"

"No. So you don't have to feel threatened."

"Threatened is definitely not how I'm feeling now. I'm just surprised. You wanted a family."

"That probably won't happen."

"You said there was nothing wrong with you."

"There isn't.'

Brow knotted, he sent a shafting glance her way. "A vicious circle, isn't it? You don't think anyone would stick with you for the long haul and you don't believe in having kids without a stable family life."

He'd been right about wanting a stable family life. But that had been then. This was now. "How are you feeling about the whole family and children thing? You weren't all that keen, I recall."

"Seven years ago, I had other plans. Kids were something vague in the future."

"And now?"

"I agree with you about a stable family life. So, nothing much has changed. I've got plenty of time."

"Once I'm out of your life."

His mouth curled. "As I said. Plenty of time."

What did that mean? Plenty of time for them to be together before he went elsewhere? Harriet curled her toes as Lucas continued to rub her foot with his. "Would you like to stay once we've eaten?"

His foot stilled, and his face tightened. "Thank you, but I should go."

Harriet bit her lip remembering how odd and silent he had been when they had made love. It obviously hadn't been what he expected. Fixing her brightest smile to her mouth she grabbed the last sandwich and bit into it. Chewing with a mouth suddenly dry, she forced herself to swallow. "I was getting greedy. Don't worry, I don't expect you to feel any obligation to hang around afterwards. It's supposed to be about having fun." Her voice wobbled a little at the end, but she hoped it was a creditable effort.

Lucas cursed himself for his lack of tact. "Don't take it that way, Harry. I just have a lot to think about and I'm used to being on my own."

With a hiccough, Harriet tried to pull away. "It's fine, really. I know it probably isn't much fun when you have to treat me like breakable china. You're probably used to woman who can be more inventive and tie themselves in knots."

"Why would I want to be with a woman who can tie herself into knots? It sounds uncomfortable. At this moment, I want to be with you."

"At this moment?"

Her soft mouth hardened as she queried his words and

Lucas cursed his stumble. "I want to be with you. Full stop. No conditions." He kissed her firmly on the lips. "Are you busy this weekend?"

"I have a rehearsal tomorrow afternoon for a demonstration a group of us are doing for a disability event in December. It should finish around five. Then Sunday I have dancing classes I help at from one o'clock until four."

He took the opportunity to kiss her again. "That leaves a perfect window of opportunity from five tomorrow to lunchtime Sunday. And then we have dinner with your parents." He kissed her one last time and gathered up his backpack. "I'll see you tomorrow after five."

It was close to six when the buzzer went. When she opened the door, Lucas was wearing jeans and a t-shirt again along with a rather grim expression. His face softened when he saw the concerned expression on hers. "Hey, Harry, sorry I'm late." Spinning away from the door, Harriet shrugged. "No problem. I've been checking my emails. What's the plan?"

Lucas perched on a stool in the kitchen as Harriet poured them each a glass of water. "I was thinking we could go and eat at Southbank and afterwards we could go back to my place. I can show you my etchings...I mean, view." His grin disarmed her, and she relaxed a fraction as he continued. "I have chocolate mud cake in the fridge. There is one catch."

Harriet eyed him warily. "What's the catch?"

"You need to let me carry you into the house. It has to be one of the most inaccessible houses in Brisbane. Down a slope and then up the steps."

Harriet sipped her water thoughtfully. "If I humiliate myself, I get mud cake? That's a hard decision Lucas Hall."

Lucas smiled a little wryly, "You could have me as well. If you still want me, that is?"

Harriet put her water down on the bench. "That could just push me over the edge. That is if I understand you correctly. Sex and mud cake are on the menu?"

Lucas watched her fingers as they ran around the rim of the glass with an odd expression on his face. "If that's how you want to look at the offer, I guess so. Not necessarily in that order."

Harriet frowned at his choice of words, but he smiled at her. Reassured, she smiled back. "It sounds good to me. Your car or mine?"

"Mine would be convenient for me. I think your chair will fit in the boot comfortably."

Harriet nodded, "I need a shower. Do you mind waiting?"

"Not at all. May I come and talk to you while you get ready?"

If Harriet thought Lucas had anything else in mind but talking, she was wrong. He did assist her with removing the braces. He seemed to find them fascinating. The rest of the time he leaned against the basin asking her about her rehearsal and talking about a project he was doing with one of the larger universities. When she finished her shower, he handed her a towel absently in the middle of telling her a humorous story about a new recruit who put down software tester as his previous job but turned out to have been a keen gamer.

"He's got potential, but we've put him on as a trainee, so he can do some background study." Harriet found herself intensely interested in what he was saying but wondered why he was telling her. He'd always talked to her about his University studies and assignments and listened gravely to her opinions. But she hardly thought he would care for her opinions now he was running his own company.

Lucas watched her dress in the bedroom using the aids she kept on the chest at the end of the bed. Once again, he had the thoughtful expression that said he was absorbing the information and processing it. When she reached for her knee braces, he stepped forward and helped her strap them on. "How many sets do you have?"

"Three, two padded sets for day to day use and the moulded ones for swimming. I sponge the padding down each night when I change them over." Picking up her towel Lucas hung it in the bathroom before re-joining her. Conscious of him watching she pulled on a pair of soft caramel trousers and a pale lavender top.

He nodded, perhaps in approval. "Nice. Are we ready to go?"

Downstairs, Lucas held the car door as she transferred to the BMW before folding the chair and putting it in the boot. When he climbed into the car, he sat quietly for a moment looking at her. The darkness in his eyes sent a ripple of something to her gut. He leaned over, avoiding the console between the seats, and she held her breath.

His fingers on her jaw created tiny frissons of sensation on her neck and throat. His lips caressed her cheek and the corner of her mouth before settling nicely on her bottom lip. "Hello," his breath mingled with hers as he whispered the greeting against her lips. His mouth lingered a moment before firming and pulling away, shifting back in the driver's seat. Harriet was torn between wishing he had kissed her like that back in the apartment and the heated awareness they never would have made it this far if they had.

**8**

———

Southbank was busy as always on a Saturday. They meandered along the boardwalk enjoying the sights and sounds of the park and river. Lucas watched Harriet manoeuvre along the cement paths, her arms working to keep up with him. The last time they'd been here together they'd held hands. It was the little things like that that tightened his throat. He'd not appreciated the simple joy of entwined fingers, palm to palm. Until there had been no-one to hold his hand. No-one to care.

Back then, it had been new to both of them. Exciting. It was hard to keep things cool making out, not wanting to stretch the limits. Needing to keep things within the boundaries set by Harriet's youth and convictions. The chemistry had been off the charts. Even lacking a comparison he'd known it was something special. Being with Harriet, he was comfortable.

She didn't laugh at him like the other girls who made fun of his awkward attempts to chat them up. When he babbled on like an idiot about some new computer development or an on-line game he played with his mates, she listened and asked questions. She made him feel a million dollars. Like he could conquer the world.

Which was why the shock of her attack hit him so hard. Why it took weeks to figure out maybe there was more to it. The only thing she hadn't belittled was his manhood. And walking in to hear her doing just that to that skeezy school friend had been the last straw.

Harriet had her taped. He'd sold Sondra the ticket in the first flush of anger and paid for it by having to fend her off all the way to L.A. There was only one person with whom he wanted to join the mile-high club. If she wasn't available, he'd stick to his computers. At least they were logical.

With a laugh, Harriet brought him back to the present.

"What's so funny?" He sat on a nearby bench and she joined him with a flourishing turn.

She stifled another laugh. "I just realised that even though this time I'm the one with the wheels, you're still getting the looks from all the girls."

"Are you looking, Harry?"

"I'm just thinking about dessert." Harriet grinned back. Her eyes sparkled, and his heart flip-flopped. When she was natural, like this, it brought everything back. He touched her hand lightly before standing up and starting to walk again. "We should think about eating. What do you fancy for your pre-dessert course?"

They chose seafood from one of the takeaways and Lucas carried the bag back to the boardwalk. They ate in a comfortable silence with occasional comments about the food and the view. A City Cat went past, and Harriet mentioned she hadn't been on one for years.

Lucas looked at her curiously because he knew they were accessible for people in wheelchairs. It had been a favourite cheap excursion on a weekend for the two of them to go along the river to Hamilton and back. She must have been conscious of his scrutiny because she smiled grimly. "Too romantic. I don't do romance anymore."

"That's a dampener for someone who has chocolate mud cake in the fridge at home."

Harriet winked at him. "Chocolate mud cake isn't about romance, it's about feeding the senses."

"Duly noted. No romantic gestures." Lucas licked his fingers. Harriet's eyes widened. He slowed down the process, sucking lightly on the end of his thumb, watching the way her pupils dilated. She wanted this thing between them as much as he did. Grabbing the serviettes to clean his hands he pushed the small sachets towards her. "You can have the cleaning wipes as you need to put your driving gloves back on."

Traffic was light as they drove back across the river to Auchenflower and Harriet was amazed when they pulled up in the driveway of a spectacular old Queenslander with wide verandas. "It's enormous, Lucas. Look at the Jacarandas. They must be a hundred years old."

Built on a large, steeply sloping block, in this obscure backstreet of the inner-city suburb, it extended over two levels. The timber top floor of the house was almost at street height while the lower level of stone was partly dug into the hillside.

Lucas pulled her chair out of the boot and carried it down the slope and up the high external staircase and placed it ready for her on the veranda. When he came back, he stood beside the car door as Harriet pulled herself up. "So, Harriet, do you trust me?"

She looked at the old cement path and the timber stairs and put her arms around his neck. "I suppose if I want mud cake, I have to."

Lucas picked her up, closing the car door with his elbow and strode along the path and up the stairs with an ease that said volumes for his fitness levels. Once on the veranda he set her down but held her against his body, supporting her weight as he nuzzled her neck. "You smell of flowers and fish and chips. The perfect woman." Harriet wriggled and gasped as he nipped her on the shoulder while lowering her into the chair. "Time for the tour, Harry. You have to earn your dessert."

On closer inspection, Harriet could see the house needed work, the paint peeling in places and scuffed timber skirting boards. The spacious rooms, high moulded ceilings and ornate trims on the doors and windows told of an era of gracious living. Lucas leading her through the house, watched her face intently as she exclaimed over each new discovery. "I've never seen a house with so many original features. How did you find it?"

"It was owned by the same family right through the last hundred years until the last member of the family died a year ago. She was a spinster with very little money, so the building escaped the usual renovations. The bathrooms were partially done in the fifties and are adequate but basic. I won't have any qualms about ripping them out and doing them up. The same with the kitchen."

"Do you have staff? There's a lot of it."

"I employ outside staff for gardening and cleaning. I'm still looking for a housekeeper to oversee everything. Graeme might know someone suitable. It has to be the right person."

"Will they live in?"

"Yes. A self-contained apartment downstairs eventually."

"You like your privacy."

"Of course."

They entered the kitchen as he spoke, and Harriet looked around curiously. A good size room with plenty of space even with the large, pine kitchen table in the middle, it was definitely in need of some help. The stove was a wood burner and Harriet wasn't surprised to see a microwave on the old, red Formica topped cupboard and a brand new stainless-steel fridge. "Don't tell me you cooked the mud cake in the microwave?"

Lucas laughed, and she hugged herself. It was a wonderful sound she'd never expected to hear again. "Wouldn't you like to know? I bought it from the Cheesecake Shop down the road. You see I reveal my secrets under your expert interrogation."

"All your secrets?" Harriet sidled up to Lucas where he was leaning on the table.

"Well, most of them anyway. Are you ready for mud cake and whipped cream?"

They sat on the back veranda to eat and Harriet had to admit the view was comparable to her own. Lucas put his arm around her shoulder to point out her apartment and left it there while they shared the dessert stroking the soft flesh just inside her collar.

"Are you enjoying this, Harry?"

Harriet swallowed another delectable mouthful with a muffled moan. "Oh yes. My taste buds are in heaven." She looked sidelong at Lucas. "There are a few other senses just asking to be tantalised as well."

"You, my lady, are a wanton woman. Are you planning to wear me out?"

Harriet licked the last of the cake and cream from her

spoon "Absolutely." Lucas stood and led the way to a part of the house Harriet hadn't seen. "This is the bedroom section. There are six but only two are habitable so far."

Harriet looked into one as they went past and recognised an old double bed with a green and gold cover. "You still have that old bed?"

"I left my stuff at Mum's place. It should do up really well for one of the bedrooms here. The right era. But I go for size and comfort these days."

Lucas paused at the end of the corridor and opened the door of the room letting Harriet enter first. The room hadn't been decorated but the king-size black and gold brass bed was obviously new. It was just as high as Harriet's bed and had a dark green quilt with stacks of pillows of all shapes and sizes in various shades of purple.

"The woman at the shop just kept adding to the pile and I didn't know how to say no." The smile that accompanied the confession was slightly embarrassed.

"I bet you didn't. I'm surprised she didn't come home with them"

He looked around sharply. "You think she was flirting?"

"Sometimes you are such a geek."

Lucas put his hands on his hips and laughed out loud at that. "Just as well I didn't notice because even with a bed this size it could have been a bit crowded. I keep chucking them in the corner but the cleaner sticks them back on the bed."

Harriet Emerson was so beautiful Lucas couldn't believe she'd ever picked him. Even though she'd discarded him just as easily. Pushing that thought away, he picked her up and carried her to the bed. He was starting to understand her reasoning but there were still questions. He watched her as she wiggled into the middle of the bed using only her arms, the movement of her arched body almost erotic. He pulled off his boots and socks and attended to hers and lay on the bed beside her. "Do you like my house?"

Harriet propped herself onto her elbows. "I love it. You were incredibly lucky to find it." She squirmed as Lucas started undoing her buttons, his tongue following the opening of her blouse. He moved straight to her trousers and dragged them down over her hips, taking the lacy undergarment with them.

The loose fabric slipped easily over the braces and soon they were hanging over the end of the bed along with his shirt. Turning his attention back to her breasts, he pushed the blouse off her shoulders and unclipped the front opening of the bra.

"You really shouldn't do that, Lucas."

He lightly ran his tongue over a nipple "And why not?"

She quivered under his touch, sending a rush of blood to heat his groin. She was a bloody electrical generator. Flick the switch and his brain was short circuiting from the surge of power.

Harriet put her hands to his jeans to undo the button and pull down the zip. "Because I'm going to have to do this." She placed her palm against him feeling the proof of his arousal, squeezing him gently.

"Hang on a minute." He tightened his abs, taking a quick breath. "Do you want to see if high beds are good for something other than falling off?"

Harriet looked up, her eyes wary. "Maybe. Does it involve pain?"

"What do you mean?"

"You have the word falling in a sentence with beds. That's not usually good."

"You really like to over think things. Isn't that my job?"

"All right, Mr. Lucas Hall. If that's how it is, my body is all yours. Only one condition."

"What's that?"

"I get to have an orgasm. You as good as promised, along with the mud cake."

"Your wish is my command."

Lucas stood and pulled off his jeans, pleased with the way her gaze lingered on his naked body. He scooped her up and turned her on the bed, so her legs dangled on the side. "Pillow?"

She grabbed one and tucked it under her head. "Are you going to tell me what's going on?"

"This is all about my fantasy, sweetheart. Do you mind?"

Harriet shook her head, his obvious excitement stirring her own as he hooked his fingers under her thighs, separating them and holding them steady against his hips with her feet dangling.

"No pain?"

"No pain."

The emerald green irises shrank to a vivid rim around the black pupil. The tremor in his body echoed in hers. He'd barely touched her and she was liquefying, readying herself for his invasion.

His erection rubbed her inner thigh and she propped herself up on another pillow.

He looked a question and she grinned, a bit wobbly. "All the better to see you with, Mr. Wolf."

Eyes gleaming with something fierce he tugged her closer. His thrust almost lifted her off the bed. He stilled, searching her face, hesitating.

"Still okay?"

He'd never been so rough before, even before the accident. But there had only been that one night, really. They'd fooled around a bit, but once they'd made up their mind to get married, they'd decided to wait. That night, after all the waiting, had been wonderful. And then everything had fallen apart. She blinked to clear her vision and focussed on Lucas.

Perspiration beaded on his upper lip and trickled down his chest. Whether it was the position, or his excitement, she'd never felt so full, so close to the edge, just from his penetration. She nodded slowly as she moved her hands to cover her tingling breasts. A huff of sound left her at the sudden spasm at her core. She chafed the sensitive tips and the muscles constricted again. Lucas looked almost feral, telling her with his smile he felt the reaction. Could feel her tightening around him.

He began to rock and almost immediately the beginnings of an orgasm started to build. When she tugged and stroked her nipples it sent a surge of liquid fuel to the fire. His grip tightened as he quickened the pace, flesh slapping against flesh in archaic rhythm. Her gasps of pleasure culminated in a cry of sheer exhilaration at the sensation of Lucas pulsing within her as he reached climax, triggering her body to convulse around him.

Sliding his hands under her hips Lucas gently pushed her back onto the bed before moving to lie beside her.

"Who said I needed someone who can tie themselves in knots? You're going to be the death of me." His fingertips stroked her cheek, the action triggering a choking sensation in her throat. "I can't resist you. I never could."

He grabbed his shirt to wipe the perspiration from his face and chest. "I need a shower."

After they showered together Lucas brought them both a large glass of water and they sprawled amongst the cushions, sipping and talking and fondling.

"Lucas?"

"Hmmm?"

"What happened about Vegas?"

"I told you. Nothing. The guys partied, we did the conference thing and went back to L.A. at the end of the week."

"I meant...You said..."

"You're wondering if I took advantage of the many delights of the showbiz, gambling, wedding and divorce capital of the U.S. of A." He rubbed one hand against his thigh as he shifted, moving away to prop himself higher on the pillows and place his glass on the floor.

"I expected to hear you'd started the divorce proceedings. But there was nothing. Only the postcard from Sondra."

"And you wondered if there was any significance."

"I suppose so." She watched as his fingers tangled, rubbing the knuckles of one hand. "Was there any significance?"

"I wasn't drunk enough to do the waking up in Vegas scenario. For anything else I would have had to stay longer." His fingers marched across the sheets to prod her ribs. "I'm not the only one who makes rash declarations and doesn't follow through."

She ducked her head to evade his accusing stare. "It's never too late."

"No. But I've got other priorities at the moment."

With a soft gasp, she twisted under his touch, as his hand cupped her breast, squeezing her nipple.

Reaching across, she put her half empty glass on the bedside table. His mouth followed the trail made by his hand and she surrendered, willing, eager, to forget the past in order to taste Lucas all over again. In the end, exhaustion lulled them into asleep, curled up together under the green quilt, the cushions scattered to the corners of the room.

Harriet woke first as the morning light trickled into the room, past old velvet swags that had seen better days. The warm smooth skin against her back felt incredibly good and the way his arm rested lightly on her hip while the other cradled her head against his shoulder triggered a feeling of contentment that was unfamiliar. She was used to filling every waking moment with activity of some kind so lying enfolded by Lucas was, at the same time, soothing and unnerving.

The hand on her hip began to move softly, stroking the skin and exploring. Harriet turned into the embrace and found herself looking into green eyes still soft from slumber. His voice was husky. "Hey, how did you sleep?"

Harriet stretched, rubbing her body against his. "So well, I can't believe it. I must have worn me out as well as you." Lucas pulled her against him and Harriet opened her lips for his kiss giving Lucas every opportunity to prove himself fully recovered. Which he duly did, to her delight.

They breakfasted on the back veranda on croissants and bacon and eggs cooked by Lucas, sharing the Sunday paper, occasionally commenting on the news of the day. She'd teased him about having a real newspaper, knowing that he used his tablet the rest of the week. He'd raised one eyebrow.

"It's more fun this way. More relaxing. It's what I need on the weekend."

It was relaxing, just sitting around, no urgency to chat and fill the silence. It had been like this the first time, long hours spent silently studying together. It had been one way of keeping their hands off each other. In hindsight, she wished they hadn't been so darn virtuous. It was good that they still had that capacity for being together comfortably. Maybe this would be what it would be like if he stayed around.

Looking at him out of the corner of her eye she noticed his attention had strayed from the newspaper. He stared into space with that grim look he seemed to get now and then. She wanted to know what he was thinking, but he turned, seemingly aware of her regard and smiled cheerfully. His eyes stayed shadowed and unfathomable giving her the feeling that he wouldn't welcome an intrusion into his thoughts.

The rules of the game were to keep it light and she was the one enforcing them, but his occasional moodiness made her nervous. "You are all right with this, Lucas?"

He put his coffee mug down and looked at her with raised brows, his eyes greener if anything. "All right with what, Harry?"

Harriet bit her lip. If she came out and said casual sex, he might think she was just using him, and it definitely wasn't that. She just knew that nothing permanent was ever going to happen under the circumstances. How would he feel if he knew the risks she was taking? She'd told him she would take care of contraception. So far there hadn't been a problem, the timing wrong. In the meantime, it was better to keep it light, so she wouldn't get in too deep again. She nearly didn't survive the first time. It was too much risk, especially with Lucas, who was the only man to ever touch her heart in that way.

Lucas watched the play of expressions on her face intently. The perky mask was slipping again and he was glad of it. "You mean am I all right with being your friend with benefits, no romance, no strings?"

Her chest rose and fell as she took a deep breath. "Yes, that's what I mean. It's just sometimes you seem a bit grim and I wondered if it was something I did. Now I mean, not seven years ago."

Folding the paper carefully Lucas placed it on the table as he contemplated her words. "You might need to define a little clearer the parameters of this relationship for me, Harriet. Are my thoughts my own or would you like me to share them? Am I entitled to probe your thoughts or are they sacrosanct?"

Harriet looked disconcerted. "Oh, I see what you mean. It's not really supposed to get that intimate is it?"

Lucas stood and came over to squat beside Harriet's chair "It's up to you, Harriet. This kind of relationship is totally new to me, so I don't know the rules." He put his hand on her thigh. "For my part I'm happy for you to ask me questions. As long as you understand I may prefer not to answer some things. Do you trust me to make that kind of call?"

"I guess so. And I suppose you can ask me things too, on the same proviso."

"Good." Steadying himself against the wheel Lucas kissed her on the lips. "Very good. Delectable even." He returned to his seat. "To answer the original question about me looking grim. No, you haven't done anything to cause it. I do tend to look grim when I'm concentrating on things. My work colleagues complain about it all the time. I will endeavour to do better."

Harriet shook her head "I suppose I just want to you tell me if I upset you or do something you don't like."

Picking up his coffee, Lucas took a sip and screwed up his nose "Cold. We have to get to know each other again. We'll probably make mistakes." He grimaced again. "Almost certainly." He stood and started stacking the plates and mugs. "It's nearly time for you to go to your class. Should I drop you home, so you can take your car?"

At the top of the steps watching Lucas return from putting her things in the car, Harriet took a long look around at the house, wondering how Lucas would decorate the lovely home. Eventually he would settle down and fill the bedrooms with children. Tears pricked as she closed her eyes trying to block out the images of Lucas surrounded by a young family.

"Are you okay?"

Lucas was bending over her and Harriet dropped her lids hoping he wouldn't see the moisture. "I'm fine. Looking forward to getting to my class this afternoon." She put her arms up and Lucas picked her up, holding her unnecessarily close.

"Whatever you say, sweetheart." He kissed her hard on the lips "One day...."

He shook his head and started down the stairs, leaving Harriet wondering what he intended to say. She settled into the car while he fetched her chair and loaded it into the boot and in a matter of minutes, they were pulling up outside her apartment block. "I can't believe we lived so close and never bumped into each other until now."

"I've only lived in this area for a few months. My apartment was in the city along the river and when I first arrived back, I stayed at my mother's place. The same with my office. It was initially in the valley and we only bought the building at Milton at the same time as I moved into the house. I don't think I did more than pass through this part of the city since I graduated."

He pulled her wheelchair out and stood beside it as Harriet climbed out of the car and arranged herself. "You'll be coming tonight?" Lucas nodded as he closed the car door and handed the purse to her.

"I'll meet you here and walk over with you, if that's okay?" Harriet agreed and with a brisk wave he climbed back in the car and was gone. In spite of his soothing words that morning, Harriet still had the feeling that Lucas in his moods was thinking about her. That moment at the top of the stairs, she sensed real frustration in his half-finished sentence. Was he getting bored with having to carry her around and do things for her? He never complained and often did things for her even when she insisted she could do them herself, but maybe the novelty was wearing off.

When they made love, there was always a touch of constraint and Harriet wondered if it was because he was always having to be careful with her not to hurt her or he was emotionally distancing himself. He had been more aggressive last night but afterwards it sounded like he resented her power to arouse him. This morning too, his responses had been cool and the look in his eyes almost antagonistic. He seemed anxious for her to leave. As if he planned to be somewhere else.

Whatever he was doing during the day he was prompt to the minute arriving outside her apartment building at ten to six with a bottle of wine in a recyclable holder. Harriet had just come down in the lift and saw him arrive as she exited the foyer. He looked gorgeous in tailored navy slacks and a long sleeved, collarless shirt in a light grey with mother of pearl buttons opened at the throat. His dark hair was slightly ruffled as if he had been running his hands through it and his green eyes glittered as he took in the low-cut jersey knit dress in a gum leaf green with gold embroidery around the collar and sleeves.

"You look good enough to eat." He stooped to kiss her on the cheek and when her hand came up to touch his jaw he planted a lingering kiss on her mouth for good measure.

"Thank you for coming, Lucas. You didn't have to." She saw his lips compress.

"I did, Harriet. I've always liked your parents. They were always very good to me all things considered."

"What do you mean all things considered?"

His lips quirked, "Considering I was a twenty-two-year-old impoverished student on a motorbike, trying to seduce their not quite eighteen-year-old, schoolgirl daughter."

"They never thought that."

He laughed cynically "They would have been right, wouldn't they? Your father at least knew exactly what I was after. You said it yourself that last day in the hospital."

Confused, she looked up at his face, disturbed by the return to grimness. "I was just saying that. I thought you understood." She sucked in a breath. "Is that how it was? You just wanted sex. I thought…"

With a long stride, he stepped in front of the chair, stopping her. "No, it wasn't like that. You know how it was. To me it was pretty damn special. I'm sorry I'm so bad tempered lately. I like to be in control and when I'm around you these days… Well I don't behave well when I don't get what I want."

"What do you want?"

He stared at her up tilted face and sighed. "I don't know, Harry. I really don't know if what I want even exists anymore. Which begs the question of course."

"What question?"

Lucas moved aside. "Of why we are even discussing this when we should be up at your parent's place."

It was strange eating with Harriet's parents, for the first time in more than seven years. They had encouraged him to come around, back then, once they'd accepted that Harriet wasn't going to drop him. Not that he took advantage of it too often. The occasional dinner and Harriet's eighteenth birthday party. She had positively glowed, her eyes sparkling with the secret knowledge they shared. All their plans wrecked in a moment. It was easy to accept now, knowing that it was her accident that had changed them, not the childish whims of a spoilt rich girl. The pain was still there, but the anger was directed at fate, rather than Harriet.

He watched her with her parents, more assured than in the past, more willing to express a contrary opinion. She was different in so many ways now. Stronger yet more vulnerable. She'd lost that air of arrogant self-assurance that had tricked him that last time. Physically she'd changed as well. Not just the injuries, but the wiry slenderness of the ballet dancer had gone. Her strength was all in the upper body, the legs weaker, muscle wasted and less toned.

Her mind? In some ways it was a closed book to him. Her determination to keep their relationship on a casual plane was frustrating. Even he, with his crap interpersonal skills could see she was aching for more. But was it more with him, or just more? More with someone who hadn't let her down in the past. Who she could trust not to run when the going got tough.

Back at her apartment, the tension between them sizzled. Slamming the door, Lucas pulled Harriet from her chair, supporting her with one arm while the other hand pulled down her straps allowing access to her breasts through the lace of her bra. Her skin was silk under his mouth, the rasp of his stubble against the lace a heady contrast.

Harriet wrapped her arms around his neck taking most of her weight and he used both arms to lift her higher, pulling her dress up before ripping open his trousers. He probed gently with his fingers and finding her ready, he pulled aside the fabric and let her slide down to take his full length. Her fingers dug into the skin at his nape, the sharp pain shooting straight to his dick. Maybe she was as desperate as he was.

She shuddered, and Lucas tightened his grip on her thighs, supporting the weight of her legs as he turned to put her back against the wall of the hallway. His mouth sought hers and his tongue delved deep, its thrust echoing the pulsing rhythm as he drove into her body. He needed this connection, if this was all she was prepared to give. Heat built in his gut, pushing him to the edge of control.

She was slick and wet with wanting, the slap of flesh against flesh sounding loud in the silence of the apartment, echoing the panting breaths and gasps. A wave of sensation shivered through him burning his skin where it touched her sweat damp skin. He was lost as she cried out, his name juddering against his mouth, her internal muscles clenching around him. The jagged rhythm sent him soaring, sublimating the pain of her teeth on his lip. He poured himself into her, pumping hard, giving all of himself, offering her everything.

Harriet didn't want to come back. She wanted to stay with Lucas in that place where nothing mattered but the connection between them. His heart pounded against her chest, a counter point to the rapid flutter of hers as they took deep breaths to bring them back down.

Straightening, he pulled back and let her slide a little, so she could drop into her chair. Harriet watched him pull up his underwear and trousers and do up the zip leaving the button and belt undone. His shirt was half un-tucked, and he automatically tidied himself and she did the same, pulling up her straps and adjusting the skirt of her dress. He had a slight frown as he looked at her, fiddling with her twisted strap.

"I'm sorry Harry. That lacked finesse."

Harriet stared back at him. "Do you see me complaining? The screaming was because it was good for me, Lucas."

His lips twisted. "I always have plans to take it slow but then I touch you and they go out the window."

Harriet turned her chair and headed for the bedroom. "Slow is good for me, now you've taken the edge off." She turned at the doorway "Are you coming?"

She watched as he ran his hands through his hair and for a moment she thought he might say no. "Of course. I'll be there in a few minutes." He smiled ruefully. "Your wish is my command, as always."

He had a small gift box in his hands when he entered

the bedroom shortly after she'd climbed into bed. Purple paper with silver ribbons.

"Happy birthday." He extended his hand with the box, looking awkward and unsure. Her heart flip-flopped as she took the present, tugging on the bow at the top.

"You didn't have to."

"It's nothing special. I wanted to give you something. I've missed a few birthdays." That awkwardness was more marked, a faint flush across his cheekbones. He was so sweet like this. He'd been the same when he'd given her a locket for her eighteenth birthday. She'd been wearing it on the night of the accident but somehow it had been lost.

The lid came off easily, exposing a tissue wrapped something. She could feel his eyes on her, the nervousness radiating from him with an intensity that should have hummed like a power grid.

"Oh." The crystal fairy, all amethyst and sparkling clear features, shocked her into silence. This was so much more than an ornament.

"I saw it and thought of you."

"It's beautiful." She cradled it in her palms, revelling in the feeling of hope that warmed her from chest to fingertips. This reminder of their first meeting had to mean something. Placing it carefully on the bedside table, she reached out to grasp one strong hand. "Thank you. I love it."

"I'm glad."

With a gentle tug, she drew him down onto the bed, wrapping her arms around his waist and resting her head on his chest. His heart beat steadily under her ear. After a momentary hesitation, he folded her into his arms and they stayed there for long minutes. Whatever they had, it was more than sex. Why else would he feel like home?

"I'd like us to go to the beach on the weekend. You said you don't have rehearsals this Saturday." Harriet looked up, surprised. Lucas had been quiet since he arrived at her apartment mid-week, looking worn out and she had respected his mood, continuing to check her emails. He came straight from work and she'd already been for her swim.

He'd told her before he left that morning not to wait for him as he had meetings that could go late. The Lasagne in the oven would keep warm until he was ready to eat. His jacket and tie lay across the back of the couch and he'd toed off his shoes under the coffee table. His socked feet had a homely look that made her heart clench. Undone buttons on his shirt showed of glimpse of tanned flesh, but he didn't look terribly relaxed.

She could see shadows under his eyes and a faint frown line between his brows. Was it work or her demands? He rarely got a full night's sleep and she considered the possibility that he might prefer to be at home.

"You look tired. You don't have to stay if you don't want to."

Undoing more buttons, Lucas shook his head. "I'd like to stay but maybe I should just sleep after I've eaten. Would you mind?"

Harriet pursed her lips "Of course I don't mind. You let me sleep when I'm tired." She shut down the laptop and moved into the kitchen. "I'll serve up now and you can get off to bed." She quickly put his meal onto a plate with cutlery and put it on the coffee table before returning to the kitchen to get her own.

Lucas ate the food in silence and Harriet flicked on the

television to watch the news channel. With a murmured thank you, he put his plate into the sink and vanished into the bedroom.

By the time Harriet finished and cleaned up it was almost nine o'clock, so she waited by the phone for the expected call. Her mother wouldn't talk long once she knew Lucas was present and Harriet wondered if they would stop calling if he became a permanent presence in her life. It was too much to hope for. She had given up suggesting to her parents that they call less often. It had been the one condition, "request", they had made when she'd insisted on her own place. It seemed a small compromise at the time. Only now was she finding it too intrusive.

Once the call was over, she turned out the lights and went into the bedroom. Lucas lay asleep on the bed in just his undershorts, his bronzed shoulders and chest bare. She could see his hair, still slightly damp from the shower, glistening in the light from the bedside lamp on her side of the bed.

Harriet had her shower and did her usual preparations before climbing into bed beside Lucas. He lay on his side facing her, his features lit by the lamp. The frown lines were smoothed away in sleep, but the shadows were still visible under the dark lashes. He really was a beautiful man. His body and the strong lines of his face constantly distracted her.

With a sigh she turned away from temptation and switched off the light. Sometime in the night Lucas put his arm over her and she could feel the smooth skin of his chest, warm against her back and she slipped contentedly into a deeper sleep, not waking until well after her usual time. Lucas was dressing, and Harriet propped herself up to watch his fingers do up the buttons and tuck his shirt in.

As if he felt her scrutiny he looked up and smiled at her and her heart did a crazy flip at the tender expression on his face.

"Morning, Harry." He walked around the bed to kiss her lips but pulled back immediately. "I have to rush. Breakfast is in the warming oven. I might see you at the game if I get away on time."

He was gone before she had a chance to reply so she got up, dressed and went to check the warming oven. Bacon, eggs sunny side up and grilled tomato with a sprig of parsley. The perfect man. Maybe too perfect, the sensible side of her brain tried to tell her.

Saturday morning and the BMW ate up the highway comfortably. Lucas checked the time complacently as they arrived in time for an early morning tea at a café at Broadbeach. He was determined to give Harriet the whole beach experience. She'd loved the surf when they were together.

He couldn't believe she hadn't been near the ocean since the accident. It seemed her life had become bound by accessibility issues. Apart from the basketball and the cinema, she didn't seem to go anywhere much socially. She'd protested at first at having to be carried but gave in at the sight of the ocean.

At Tallebudgera Creek they hired a canoe and shared the paddling as they explored the estuary. Lunch at Burleigh Heads was followed by a visit to the beach at Coolangatta. Lucas hired a longboard and surfed while Harriet lazed on the beach in a bikini watching his prowess like any surfer chick. Now he just had to get her into the water.

"Are you ready?"

She glanced at her phone. "Is it time to leave?"

"Time to swim."

"I couldn't. Not in the surf. It's too rough."

He scooped her up and tossed her over his shoulder. "No such word…"

"Are you insane? Put me down."

"You didn't say the magic word."

"Please. Please put me down."

"Okay."

She squealed as he lowered her into the water, but suddenly she was laughing. He helped her onto the board and pushed it out through the breakers until they reached the relatively calmer waters away from the other surfers. Steadying himself, he pulled himself up on the board facing her, letting his legs dangle in the water.

Harriet let her legs slide off the board so they were knee to knee. "I haven't been out on the ocean like this since…" Her gaze shifted to the horizon briefly before returning to his face. "Since you brought me here when we were first dating."

Lucas rubbed his hands along her thighs until they rested on her hips. "Are you glad you came?"

Harriet smiled her eyes glowing "Oh yes. It's been a wonderful day. It's funny. When I've thought about the beach before, it's always been too hard and too complicated. But today, with you, everything has been so easy."

She leaned forward to kiss him and he responded, licking the salt from lips that burned as they touched. The board wobbled and they both laughed as Lucas slipped into the water so he could steady it.

Exhausted but happy, Harriet slept most of the way home, only waking as Lucas carried her inside her unit to the bathroom. He had already brought her chair and their beach towels up while she slept, so he helped her strip off, ready for the shower, putting her light swimming braces on the bench beside her. Refreshed by her nap and stimulated by the shower, Harriet helped Lucas remove his board shorts pleased to see he was demonstrating a distinct interest as she started to soap his body.

Reaching down he lifted her up, hands gripping her thighs behind her knees, as he usually did, holding her weight easily. Harriet wrapped her arms around his shoulders, taking some of her weight. She buried her face in his throat, hiding from laughing eyes that seemed to see everything. He hitched her higher, shifting his grip.

Caught unawares, she screamed. In a haze of pain, she saw Lucas' horrified face as his fingers tightened on her legs. "My knee. The right one. I've twisted it," she gasped out, fighting back tears.

Lucas pulled her out of the shower still dripping and carried her to the bed. "What do I need to do? Ambulance?"

Harriet moaned "Not the ambulance."

Lucas turned off the shower, grabbed some towels and dried her swiftly being careful not to put pressure on the knee. He pulled the doona over her to keep her warm and winding a towel around his waist he left the room.

"I'm just getting the icepacks from the freezer." Wrapping them in a towel he placed them against the injured knee, his face grave. "Do you want to go to the emergency room? I can take you."

He sat on the side of the bed and smoothed the hair back from her pallid face, mopping the tears with the corner of his towel.

"I'm sorry. I didn't mean for this to happen."

He kissed her forehead. "I know you didn't. I'm just as much as fault. I forgot about your braces."

An hour later they were sitting in a treatment room at the Mater hospital waiting for the registrar to arrive. Lucas had helped her dress and driven her to the hospital without complaint, but Harriet worried about the thoughtful expression on his face. Twice she had said something to him and he had brought his attention back to her with an effort, his smile absent as he listened to her repeat her comment.

When the registrar entered the room, Lucas watched silently as the young doctor greeted her with easy familiarity.

"Well, well, well. It's been a good while since we've had you in here. What did you do this time? Basketball aerobatics again?"

Harriet blushed and the doctor glanced over at Lucas curiously. "It doesn't look like you've thrown anything out too far, but we'll have you in Monday for a scan. In the meantime, absolutely no weight bearing. On either leg. You don't want to injure the other one by pushing it too far."

He was strapping the knee as he gave further instructions and advice on painkillers. In response to Harriet's query he smiled. "I don't think you should have a problem doing the demo next weekend. If it's still tender just keep weight off it. Stick to the wheelchair even for around the house."

Back at her apartment they ate the takeaways they picked up on the way home.

He was restless, stalking the room like a panther. "You'll need help for the next few days."

"I'll be fine, Lucas. I've been through this before."

He stopped pacing and stood awkwardly with his hands

in his pockets. "Of course. Is there anything I can do to help?"

"No more than what you usually do. I only really need help in the shower for the transfer. I'm actually strong enough to do all the other transfers just using my arms."

Lucas nodded. "I'm supposed to be in Sydney on Monday and Tuesday, but I can cancel."

Harriet stilled as she heard something in his voice that disturbed her. "It's just a shower, Lucas. Mum can help me for a couple of nights. It's hardly worth cancelling a business trip for. I can work from home for a few days."

He looked relieved and a little guilty and Harriet knew at that moment he had finally realised the trap being with a person with a disability could become.

She trailed off to bed while Lucas tidied up and when he climbed into the bed, she stayed on her side instead of snuggling as she usually did. When he made no move to touch her either, she had a feeling this was the beginning of the end.

On Sunday he insisted she do nothing from the moment she woke up to him returning from the shops with coffee, hot chocolate and a range of bakery items for breakfast. After breakfast he settled her on the couch and they read the Sunday newspapers together pointing out things of interest and swapping sections. It was nice, but Harriet could feel his restraint. There were no more casual touches and caresses, stolen kisses, only impersonal support when she needed assistance.

Lucas made a salad for lunch and she was grateful for his quick thinking when her parents turned up unexpectedly at afternoon tea time, cake in hand. He grabbed a sarong for her to wrap around over her shorts to hide the medical strapping on her knee. He wouldn't let her help with cooking dinner either, whipping up a stir fry which they ate on the veranda. By the time he had helped her into bed she was snappy and when he offered to get her a drink, she let her frustration loose.

"I don't need a carer, Lucas."

She regretted it immediately when Lucas withdrew silently, his face cold. When he didn't come to bed she had to bite her lip to stop herself crying. Lucas was gone in the morning when she woke up regretfully from a dream of him kissing her like there was no tomorrow and telling her he loved her. She knew he had an early flight, but Harriet wished he had woken her to say goodbye and maybe even make her dream come true. Well the kiss anyway. The other would stay in the realms of fantasy.

The next few days dragged and when Lucas came over on Wednesday night obviously exhausted Harriet ruined their reunion by telling him he should go home to bed which he did. As he had been on the verge of telling her something when she had interrupted him, he simply shut his mouth and left.

He didn't turn up at basketball on Thursday. When she got home there was a message from Lucas to say something had come up and he would come over Friday. She was to let him know if it wasn't okay. Resisting the temptation to ring up and tell him it wasn't and get the whole thing over with, Harriet went to bed, only to toss and turn as she had done all week. Stupid to sleep better when there was someone to hold you while you slept.

He was early. Lucas knew Harriet would have barely arrived home, but somehow, he'd finished early. Probably by driving his team into near rebellion. They were no doubt glad to be rid of him so they could go to the pub for their Friday night wind-down drinks. He knew better than to join them, especially after the week they'd had, putting up with his short temper. He'd apologised, but it didn't make him feel any better.

Harriet buzzed him in and he let out a breath. She was pulling away since the injury to her leg. So certain he would run. Which, given his history, she had every right to believe. He'd been at fault too, this week, nervous about hurting her, hating to see her in pain. That guilt had been riding him all week, along with some problems with the contract down in Sydney.

Banks were the worst customers, needing the highest level of security for the product, yet always with an eye to the profits. In some ways, government was easier but came with a different set of problems.

The door opened, and Harriet was there, backing away, a wary gleam in her lovely eyes. He slammed the door behind him and leaned over her in the chair, bracing himself with a grip on her wheels "How's your knee?" he murmured, his lips brushing against her ear.

"Much better."

"Good. I've missed you Harry. You won't believe how much." He kissed her, probing her mouth with his tongue desperate to take possession. She responded, parting her lips and relief washed through him, easing the pain in his chest. Pushing her backwards towards the bedroom he kept his lips moving over hers and Harriet reached up, unbuttoning his shirt and by the time they were in the bedroom she was tugging at his jeans.

God, he loved her. Still loved her. He stiffened at the

unwelcome revelation and she looked up at him, her eyes wide. Shaking his head to clear it, he dragged up a smile.

"Ready?"

Lifting her from the chair he carried her to the bed before stripping to his undershorts and joining her. He kissed her eyes and her ears, sipping at her skin and inhaling the long familiar floral scent that clung to her.

"God, I've missed this. I want to touch and taste every part of you." It had been seven long, dry years. The loving they'd shared in the past few weeks could never assuage the hunger from that drought.

He pushed the aching memories aside, focussing on the woman in front of him. If sex was all she would give him, he would take it. He paid special attention to her neck and shoulders as his shaking fingers undid the buttons on her shirt and the clip of her bra, so he could kiss her breasts and tease her nipples until they stood in stiff peaks. Her skirt barely slowed him down and he pulled it and her lace underwear down in one movement and slipped her sandals off to drop them on the floor beside the bed.

Harriet saw the moment when some unwelcome thought paralysed him. He recovered quickly enough, but the disquiet lingered. His hands lit small fires as they stroked their way back up her legs and to her inner thighs followed by his lips. He tasted her deeply, his tongue measuring broad strokes that caused her to arch into him. His long fingers probed her secrets and in moments Harriet was going up in flames unable to control the convulsions as she cried out his name in ecstasy. Waves of pleasure rolled through her, the aftershocks leaving her trembling.

As she came down from the heights, Lucas lay his head on her stomach and Harriet stroked the soft hair back from his face. His hand cupped her hip and his thumb stroked the ridge of hip bone where the veins lay close to the surface.

For a while Harriet wondered if he had gone to sleep, the slight movement of his thumb the only signifier of his alertness. Then he sighed and moved to lie beside her on the bed, placing one hand on her stomach as if to maintain contact.

"Not a very coherent greeting Harry. But I hope you realise how pleased I am to see you."

Harriet put her hand over his. "I missed you too, Lucas."

They showered together before preparing Spaghetti Bolognese from ingredients in the bag Lucas had dumped in the hallway when he arrived. The rest of the evening they spent making love with an almost frenetic desperation. She had a horrible feeling that things were reaching a climax. All the same, Harriet slept soundly in his arms until Lucas woke her up long after dawn with a sensual invitation that she had no will to resist.

All too soon it was time for Harriet to prepare for her final rehearsal, for the demonstration her group was giving that night.

Lucas was reluctant to let her out of bed. "I wish I didn't have this function to attend tonight. If it wasn't business related, I would call it off."

Harriet hushed him. "It's all right. I'm busy tonight anyway. We can see each other tomorrow."

She sent him off with a lingering kiss before heading for her rehearsal. Maybe she had been wrong about him distancing himself earlier. He certainly hadn't been at all distant last night.

**9**

———

This was a mistake. His gut told him in no uncertain terms he would regret coming. It felt all wrong being here with Angela. A glimpse of several people in wheelchairs at the Ministers table early in the evening had confirmed what he already knew. It should be Harriet at his side. Angela was charming and beautiful in her slinky red dress and strappy heals, her blonde hair piled high.

But Lucas found himself wondering about Harriet and what she was doing with her dance group. He hadn't made the connection until he'd realised the particular focus of tonight's event. If only he could be sure.

She hadn't said and with things the way they had been the last few days, he hadn't asked. He should have asked. Should have made some attempt to breach the barrier she kept between her life and their time together. Moving around the dance floor with Angela he responded to her chatter absently and when the music stopped for the compeer to announce a special event, he was more than happy to move to the side of the floor.

Another hour or two and he could politely end the evening. The crowd jostled for position, so he rested a hand on Angela's waist to keep her from being swept away.

"Ladies and gentlemen, the Minister has invited three medal winning couples from previous state Wheelchair Ballroom Championships to give a special demonstration here tonight."

Lucas strained forward to see the three wheelchair dancers and their partners come onto the floor. Sure enough, he recognised the third couple. Black hair slicked back and wearing a formal suit, he hardly knew Jimmie. So that was the out of work connection. Dressed in lavender and white with the sporting wheelchair trimmed with ribbons of the same colour, she looked quite different.

Smiling to himself, he started formulating a teasing comment about the bouffant hairstyle and heavy makeup. There was an audible murmur of appreciation from the crowd as the music started and the wheelchairs began spinning. Lucas joined in the spontaneous applause, seeking out the couple in purple.

All three couples were spectacular, but Lucas found himself watching Harriet as she spun and dipped around her male partner. Her arms were graceful and expressive and brought back to Lucas the night he had watched her perform her final ballet concert as the Fairy Queen only weeks before the accident.

A shiver prickled his spine as the memories and the reality of Harriet doing her dancing from a wheelchair came home to him. Angela must have felt the tremor, moving closer to take his arm as the performance came to a close. Jimmie, resplendent in a dark purple suit, stood beside Harriet, beaming from ear to ear at the applause.

They moved to follow their fellow dancers but the

surge of people onto the floor forced them towards his side of the room. Lucas could see her laughing and chatting to Jimmie as she made her way through the crowd and knew the moment she spotted him. Her eyes lit up and she redirected her chair, manoeuvring adroitly through the crowd.

"You came to watch after all. How lovely…"

Her voice trailed off as she saw Angela clinging to his arm and with a sick feeling in his gut, he saw her smile die, replaced by an anxious crease. Her mouth moved silently as she stared, her face leaching of colour. He started towards her, but it was too late. The stricken look on her face told it all before she made an attempt at getting it under control, with a smile that wavered before it firmed into that fake expression he hated.

"We have to go. Lovely to see you. Come, Jimmie, we need to get our gear." She spun away, and the crowd parted to let her through, closing up behind her. With a puzzled look, Jimmie waved at Lucas before vanishing in the sea of people.

Excusing himself, Lucas plunged into the crowd, but was hindered by the music starting again and more people moving onto the floor. By the time he got to the foyer Harriet was nowhere in sight. The closing of a lift door caught his eye. Taking a chance, he took the stairs, stopping at each level to see if she emerged. He was lucky at the second level, spotting Jimmie stowing the decorated chair in the red Focus.

Harriet sat in the driver's seat, hooking up her regular chair. Lucas came to a halt, panting slightly from his headlong run down the stairwell. She sat stony faced in the car refusing to look at him and Jimmie stood awkwardly beside the boot watching the confrontation.

"Harry, it isn't what you are thinking." He bent over, his hands on his thighs trying to draw breath.

Harriet pulled the lever to set the chair lift moving and was obscured from his sight for a few moments as the mechanism pulled the chair onto the roof of the vehicle. A sparkle of something under the car caught his eye. Something dropped in the rush to escape him? The chair settled on the roof with a dull clunk and a whirr of the mechanism, drawing his attention up to the girl in the car. She sat with her hands resting on the steering wheel staring straight ahead.

"Harriet, please talk to me. It was organised weeks ago before you and I were together."

"It doesn't matter, Lucas. We never said anything about exclusivity, did we? It worked out well all round, the crip gets laid and you still get to dance the night away with a real date. It's a pity the two worlds collided tonight. You should have warned me. It could have been quite embarrassing." Her face was pale but composed as she turned to look at him and Lucas was deathly afraid of the look in her eyes.

"I never wanted it to be like that, Harry. I never thought of you like that. Give me a chance to explain. Can I come over later?"

Her voice came out flat. "I don't think so. What would your date think? We've run our course, Lucas. We live in different worlds now, so it was always going to be nothing more than a nice little interlude."

Lucas put his hand on the car door to prevent her closing it. "Please, Harriet, I made a mistake. Don't write me off again. Give me a chance to fix things."

Harriet tugged at the door. "There isn't anything worth fixing. Let me go. I have to take Jimmie home."

"Wait. You forgot something." She hesitated as he went

down on one knee. He reached under the car to grab the bejewelled stiletto shoe.

For a moment something softened in her eyes as he held out the shoe. Her lashes lowered to fan out over her pale cheeks as her lips moved soundlessly once more. But he couldn't read the words.

"Harry?"

Her jaw tightened as she opened her eyes. "No more fairy tales."

Tossing the shoe into the back seat, she reached once more for the door handle.

Standing up he released it and stepped back. "Please, Harry, don't do this."

Harriet pulled the door shut, hoping to block out the desperation in his voice. Lucas looked totally defeated and her savaged heart was already painful enough. If she listened, she would give in and then it would start all over again. The futile hoping, the dreams of a future would only come crashing down again when reality reared its ugly face. It had already gone too far, the biting pain in her chest all too real. Friends with benefits had been a poor illusion.

Harriet backed out of the car park, trying not to look at Lucas as he stood there, shoulders slumped and face distraught. When she reached the turn to the exit, she could still see him in her rear vision mirror, standing there, one hand covering his eyes.

She clenched her hand over the steering knob and concentrated on her driving. If she could get home before this pain in her chest exploded...Breathing deep she focused hard on the traffic. She would be alright. Already the pain was easing, a numbness, familiar and comforting settling in the hollow of her chest.

Jimmie remained tactfully silent all the way home and she said goodnight and thanked him for his help when she dropped him off at his tiny flat. At home, Harriet had a shower before sitting at the dressing table looking at herself. Her mobile phone rang and rang, and she let it ring out. It rang three more times before whoever it was gave up. She couldn't bear to listen to Lucas justifying himself. She deleted the messages without listening to them.

Picking up the brush she began to brush her hair but stopped after only a few strokes. She'd forgotten to wash it. The hair tangled from the thick hair spray she used to keep it in place for the dancing. Exchanging the brush for a pair of surgical scissors she cut the tangles out and then kept cutting. The reflection in the mirror blurred and she widened her eyes to hold back the tears. The scissors jammed on the bunched-up hair and she tugged them loose, lying them on the dressing table. She was so tired.

Suppressing a yawn, she went to bed and slept. The mobile phone ringing shortly after eight in the morning dragged her from sleep. Heart pumping, she turned it off and buried her head in her pillows when the landline in the lounge room began ringing. It was never going to stop. She staggered out, holding onto the walls and furniture and pulled it out. In the blissful silence that followed, she crawled onto the couch.

The sound of someone in the kitchen woke Harriet and she stretched and yawned before spotting her father making himself a cup of coffee. She was really going to take back the key card. This was getting ridiculous. Only now was not the best time to try and prove she was an adult.

"Would you like a hot chocolate?"

She nodded. "Yes, please. I don't remember when I last ate." She brushed some loose hairs off the couch and a memory had her putting her hand to her head. "Oh damn." That wasn't the only stupid thing she'd done last night.

Jack brought her over the hot chocolate and she sat up to drink it.

"It was a knot. Really, I'm all right."

Just a little teensy bit heart-sore but that's normal isn't it. Harriet could tell her father was worried and she hated the fact it was her actions that put the strained expression on his face.

"Lucas rang me, Harriet. He said you'd given him the flick. He's been trying to ring and getting no answer. He came around, but no-one answered the buzzer. He was worried about you."

Harriet pointed to the phone. "That's why I unplugged them. I meant to plug them back in tonight, but I fell asleep. He only wants to justify himself, so I'm not interested."

"What had he done that was so terrible?"

"Only dated a beautiful blonde called Angela without telling me. She was glued to his side when I saw them at the IDD ball last night. He was dating her when we first met again, and it looks like he never stopped all the time he was with me."

"Did Lucas have an explanation?"

Harriet snorted. "Only that it was organised before we got together. But in that case, why didn't he tell me? Or even dump her and take me. I'll tell you why. Because he doesn't want any of his friends to see me with him. He's ashamed of me. I'm all right to have sex with but not fit to be seen in public."

A startled murmur from her father stopped her diatribe in mid flow.

"Damn. Too much information."

Harriet leaned forward to touch her father's knee. "Don't blame Lucas. I wanted it. You don't have to get the shotgun out." She sighed as she tried to get her legs comfortable "This is so unnatural isn't it. I mean a twenty-five-year-old actually mentioning her sex life to her father."

"It's probably better than talking to your mother."

Harriet groaned. "She'd be rabid."

"More than rabid. We might not mention it, hey. Or the reason for the haircut."

"You think she'll notice?"

"It's fairly...radical."

"Not good?"

He ruffled the short strands. "It actually looks quite nice, apart from the jagged bits. Shows off your eyes."

"Think of all the time I'll save brushing it. Shampoo will last for way longer."

"That's my girl. What will you do about Lucas?"

"He wanted to explain but I wouldn't listen. Pretty stupid, huh?"

"Give him a chance. If it turns out you're right and he is in a relationship with her you can let go gracefully. If not... well it's up to you to decide."

"The voice of reason. No wonder they pay you the big bucks." She ran her fingers through her hair, laughing wryly when several clumps came away in her hand. "If he rings, I'll listen. But if he doesn't, I'll know it's over."

"You don't want to be pro-active?"

"I don't want to push him. If he really is involved with

her, I don't want him to feel pressured to come back. As it is, I think half the reason why he hung around was out of pity and a smidgen of guilt. That's not my idea of a good basis for a relationship."

"I'll leave it at that."

The next day Harriet went to the hairdresser and got a haircut. A short spikey cut that sat close to her scalp. There was no other option because she'd cut some patches so short. It had taken her a while to convince her father she would be all right. The whole hair cutting thing didn't help and frankly, Harriet couldn't even explain it to herself. But it brought back bad memories for her parents, reminding them of the aftermath of the accident. It was up to her to mitigate the damage by proving she was still in control.

Lucas didn't ring again. She tried to tell herself it was for the best, but her fingers itched to call him. Her father didn't say anything, just grunting when she told him there'd been no contact. She wondered if he was disappointed, but he gave nothing away. They had always got on well and this time round it seemed no different.

Lucas really had been perfect. The perfect lover and now the perfect businessman. The kind of man any father would want as a son-in-law. But his future would have been stunted if Lucas had stayed around after her accident. Sometimes she wondered what might have happened if the accident hadn't occurred, but there was no chance of a do-over, so it was a futile exercise.

As the weeks passed and no contact came from Lucas, Harriet knew her decision had been the right one. If he really cared he wouldn't have given up so easily. In her right mind, she knew differently. He'd gone because she'd pushed him away again. Harriet punished herself by imagining all the possible scenarios in which the beautiful, long legged Angela was present on his arm or in his arms.

Christmas came and among the cards received at work was one from Lucas's company which was personally signed by Lucas in his bold writing below the standard greetings. Harriet had to resist the temptation to keep the card for herself when Jimmie recognised the name and pinned it proudly on the notice board.

The youth had met Lucas at a function he attended for one of the other charities he was involved with and Lucas told him he intended spending Christmas in London with his brother. She wondered what his mother was doing. It seemed strange.

Christmas was quiet, with just her parents on the day and a family thing with some cousins on Boxing Day. Probably just as well as the constant round of functions left her exhausted and lethargic.

The doctor's appointment was long overdue, but she couldn't evade her responsibilities forever. She'd known the risks she'd been taking.

"It's going to be difficult." He'd been her doctor since childhood. He knew her history. She trusted him.

Harriet nodded. "I know."

"Your legs wont cope with the extra weight. You'll need help. Do you have a partner? The father?"

She sucked in a breath. "He's not around."

The doctor looked at her thoughtfully, tapping his pen on the desk. "Will you be notifying him?"

Guilt wound a noose around her throat. She shook her head. "He's moved on."

"In that case, you'll need to make arrangements for

support. I suggest you give up work before the sixth month. You don't want to put too much strain on your body." He handed her a printout. "You'll need a scan."

"For the baby?"

"And your legs. You are still at risk of further aneurisms. This pregnancy will put a strain on the circulation in your lower body. We'll need to monitor it closely."

"Whatever it takes." She hugged the sheet of paper to her chest. There was no way she would risk this child. It was her last chance, her only chance.

If she could have danced out of the surgery, she would have. The only cloud on the horizon was Lucas. He would have to be told. But not yet. Not until later. When the baby was born would be soon enough. There were too many risks to navigate to ensure this baby made it safely into the world.

She would have to tell her parents. They would want to mollycoddle her. Her mother would want her to move back home, but that wasn't happening. There were other options. She had savings. If necessary, she could employ someone. She was about to be a parent. It was time to be a grownup.

"You miss Lucas."

It wasn't a question and Harriet looked over at her mother, surprised at her bringing up a subject that had been ignored for weeks.

"Yes."

"I'm sorry if anything we did drove him away."

Harriet shook her head. "It was inevitable. Nothing you said or did would have made a difference."

"You still love him, don't you?"

"Why wouldn't I. He was the only person ever to want me for me, not for what I could offer."

She was aware her mother flinched, but it was hard to care. She felt sick to her stomach.

Her mother's voice was soft, tentative. "He wanted…"

"Don't start with the whole 'boys only want sex' thing again. Of course, he wanted it. I wanted it to. It's perfectly normal for people who care about each other." She rubbed her eyes, angry at the way the tears came so readily. Stupid hormones. "Can't you understand? All I want is to be normal. Ordinary."

"You'll never be ordinary, Harriet. You're exceptional."

"So why doesn't he want me?" She sniffed inelegantly. "Why won't he fight for me? Why did he need someone else, a walking, talking Barbie doll?" Which was unfair. The woman was a lawyer. It was the walking thing she envied.

"Did you fight for him?" Her mother held up a thin veined hand. "No. I'm not talking about after the accident. You did what we all thought was best at the time."

"Dad said I should have listened this time."

"Your father is a wise man. A patient man. Your Lucas is much younger. It's hard for them to be patient."

"And I'm a sad pathetic loser feeling sorry for myself. I can do better. I will do better. Lucas may be gone but I have to get on with things."

"I know we haven't always seen eye to eye, Harriet. But your father and I only want what's best for you."

"I know. I'm a selfish brat."

"It's not about selfishness."

Harriet looked at her mother, wishing she didn't have to disappoint her again. "I'm pregnant."

10

Things were largely back to normal by the end of January and she was congratulating herself on keeping her life nicely under control when at five minutes to nine on a Friday night she answered the phone to find Lucas on the other end.

"Harriet don't hang up. I need to tell you something…ask you something."

Her heart thumped madly, and she gripped the phone with trembling fingers. She'd thought this would never happen. That she'd never hear his voice. Not until she contacted him, if and when their child was born.

He sounded odd and Harriet wondered if her parents knew he was encroaching on their time-slot. "I'm listening, Lucas. But be quick, you know I'm expecting a call."

He drew a breath that was clearly audible through the line.

"I'm going away on business for three months and I want to see you before I go. Just a cup of coffee or chocolate and it can be wherever you want."

"Three months. How will your mother handle that?"

The line went dead, except for a soft whisper that could be someone breathing.

"Are you still there, Lucas?"

"Mum passed on a few weeks before Christmas."

Harriet was silent, processing the news. It must have been almost straight after the breakup. Maybe that was why he hadn't persisted. He would have had enough on his plate. Despising herself for the hope that wiggled its way into her heart she searched for words.

A phone call wouldn't have taken that long. For either of them. *I could have been there for him. Comforting him.* If he'd wanted her. She'd worn out his patience by not responding when he reached out. Yet here he was, reaching out again.

"Harriet? I'm sorry if it's a shock. I told you her heart was dodgy."

Poor Lucas. She had the strangest urge to reach out and hug him. The relationship with his Mum had been tricky but she was still family. He'd uprooted his life in the U.S. for her. Would this mean he would be leaving again? Not just for a few months but forever. What else did he have to keep him here? Pain twisted through her chest. Not her. Yes, he was calling. But at the worst possible time.

"I sorry for your loss. Could you pass on my condolences to your family?"

"Thank you. I'll do that. When can we meet?"

What could she say? The words that wanted to spill out of her would only make things worse. It would all be for nothing and he would come to hate her. After seeing the cost to his parents, he would never want to stay married for those reasons. To be trapped into it. Especially when it might not happen. She rubbed her stomach in apology. "I'm sorry, Lucas. I just can't."

"You could come with me."

She could barely breath at the sudden hope that blossomed. Holding the phone to her chest, she quickly pulled it away, afraid he would hear the pounding of her heart. Stomping it down with a good dose of common sense, she put the phone back to her ear. Travel was out anyway.

"I can't..." It sounded so bald, so...weak. "Please, travel safely." She hung up before he could respond.

The legal papers arrived almost a fortnight later. The note from Lucas was brief and to the point. "This should have been taken care of seven years ago. Your father can advise you or refer you to a divorce lawyer. I think you will find the settlements are fair. Lucas."

Harriet stared at the signature, her chest tight and achy.

Sucking in a breath to ease the pain, she skimmed through the documents and found the part about money. He was worth a fortune. If she signed the documents as they stood, she would be worth a fortune too. Which would be totally unfair to Lucas. Her father wouldn't agree, knowing about her pregnancy. But he didn't know the whole truth and these documents would make it very clear how she had failed them all those years ago.

Her mother was still stressed over the baby. She couldn't push her further. If she had another breakdown, like before, Harriet would never forgive herself. It was over two months until Lucas would be home again. Time enough to see how things panned out with her mother. It was still early days and there was no guarantee she would carry this child to term anyway. Better to wait. She put the documents in her desk drawer and locked it. A lot could happen in a few months.

A week after he returned from his extended sojourn, Lucas resumed jogging along the river walk. Despite the early hour, there were quite a few people walking or running, including a familiar figure he didn't expect. Slowing down, he turned to confirm that it was Jack Emerson and came to a halt, waiting for the older man to catch up.

"Hi, Jack. A beautiful autumn morning in sunny Brisbane."

Jack slowed and put his hands in the pockets of his tracksuit. "So, you're back in the country. Have you seen Harriet?"

Not the most enthusiastic of greetings and Lucas could understand why. "I didn't think that would be a good idea. She was quite explicit about what she wanted last time I saw her."

Jack turned away to lean on the railing, overlooking the river, "You let her send you away twice now, lad. I expected more stamina from you, this time. The pair of you seem doomed to repeat your mistakes."

The criticism stung. "I thought you'd be pleased. You weren't happy about me being back in her life. Now I'm out again and you still aren't happy. It was Harriet's choice after all."

Jack sighed "I'm sorry, Lucas. It's not fair of me to put it all on you. Harriet is a stubborn young woman. You probably remember that from the way she fought to be allowed to date you when she was in high school."

Lucas felt a stinging in his eyes and the river blurred. He pinched the bridge of his nose and turned to Jack. "What do you think I should do?"

"That's up to you. You need to know what you want

before you go anywhere near Harriet. There are complications now."

"Complications?"

The older man shrugged. "Health things. Nothing serious. Her mother and I are there for her, so you don't need to worry. And Harriet's much stronger now than she was first time round."

With that Jack moved away at a determined pace and Lucas was left confused....and curious. For Lucas, the months away had hardened his resolve to put the past behind him and move on. Harriet had always been an impossible dream and with so much painful history between them, it probably was futile to ever hope they could make things work.

Even though he'd come to understand her rejection at the time of the accident, it was still a wound that didn't bear probing. And his own stupidity had been the reason Harriet had thrown up all the barriers again. Jack had said she was much stronger now than the first-time round. *The first time of what?*

There were still things Lucas felt were hidden from him about Harriet's recovery. Her parents were so guarded when they spoke about that time and still very protective. It niggled him because they were also supportive of her independence. But only so far.

Health issues. A cold sensation settled in his gut. He couldn't leave it at that.

Cornering her in her workplace was something Lucas wanted to avoid but needs must when the devil drives. There was still unfinished business.

The murmur of voices greeted him as the lift door opened. Jimmie stood by the reception desk talking to Harriet, who wore a bright purple flowing top over loose lilac slacks and matching crocheted beanie. Jimmie saw him and smiled, giving him a wave. Lucas held his breath as Harriet turned. She appeared thinner around the face and with her hair hidden under the beanie she looked like a child.

As he watched, her hands rested briefly on her stomach before dropping to the wheels, spinning the chair away and down the hall. Startled by what he had seen, Lucas hesitated before striding over to Jimmie.

"I need to see Harriet."

Jimmie stood his ground, his face flushed. "Harriet has to make some important phone calls. She's not available to visitors today."

Lucas backed off, forcing himself to smile at the receptionist. He had no authority to enter the private offices of the organisation. It wouldn't be fair to the young receptionist to push, to take out his anger on him. He fought back the nausea, clenching his fists to stop the betraying tremble.

"You're a good man, Jimmie. How's everything going?"

"It's okay. Harriet's training a new girl who is really nice."

"What about you, things going all right for you."

"Yes, Harriet takes me to the movies on Thursdays now she can't play basketball. We take turns to choose which movie."

"How is Harriet?" Lucas tried to keep his tone nonchalant, but Jimmie still looked anxiously down the corridor before answering.

"She's good. It's going to be different with her not around so much."

With a sigh Lucas accepted the inevitable and after chatting about general things with Jimmie to put him at his ease, he took his leave.

It had to be his child. No wonder she'd refused to see him. She must have been already showing when he called her before his overseas trip. Rage fought with fear, churning his stomach and heating his blood. The tightness in his chest wouldn't go away. What the hell was she thinking?

It was time to ask for help.

Back in his office, he dialled the Emerson's number. Caro answered, recognising his voice immediately. "Lucas? Is everything all right?"

He wondered at the urgency in her tone. "No, everything is fine. I'm just having trouble contacting Harriet and wondered if I could come talk to you and Jack tonight."

Caro paused, and he heard her sigh. "Yes, yes of course. You know where we are. We'll see you around seven."

At seven o'clock Lucas pressed the buzzer at the Emerson's apartment block, his gaze wandering to the neighbouring building two doors along. He couldn't see much of her apartment apart from the bathroom light shining. She was at home. Caro saved him from temptation by answering the buzzer and he was on his way up to the ninth floor in no time. He had only been here the once with Harriet, but it was so similar to her apartment building he was sure it was built by the same design and construction company.

Caro was alone when she let him into the apartment and she led him into the lounge room with the usual enquiries about health and work. He let her get them coffee because he could see that would make her more comfortable and when she sat with him in the lounge, he could see she was still uncertain.

It had been Caro who had fretted about his relationship with Harriet all along. In the end she'd been proved right. It probably didn't comfort her. She was a genuinely nice person. Loved her daughter devotedly.

"Jack is just over at Harriet's place trying to talk sense into her."

"About what?"

She took a sip of the coffee before answering and Lucas could sense the ambivalence about his visit "We're trying to persuade her to move back in with us."

"Why, Caro? Is she unwell?"

She looked a little hunted at that. "No not really. Just changed circumstances. You know she is giving up her job next month?"

"I got that impression from Jimmie when I spoke to him today."

"You were there? Did you see Harriet?"

"Only at distance. But I saw enough. She's pregnant, isn't she?"

Putting the cup down the woman stood abruptly "Yes she is. That's why she needs to come home. The extra weight is playing havoc with her knees."

Lucas expelled a breath at the confirmation of his fears. "She needs assistance with the transfers now?"

"Yes. The pregnancy is exacerbating the situation because the hormones are loosening up her ligaments anyway. The extra weight was always going to be a problem without that complication."

"How far along is she?" He was surprised at how much the answer meant to him, though in his heart he already knew.

"Six months. She's due in August."

"The child is mine."

"Yes, I'm afraid so, Lucas."

"She told me she was protected." Caro turned sharply and something in her face told him the answer though she didn't speak. "Actually no, I just assumed she was. She told me she would take care of it. She had to know she could fall pregnant."

"She can't take hormonal medication because of the risk of embolisms, so if she told you she was safe, she was lying."

Another lie. "Why would she risk a pregnancy with someone she didn't plan on keeping around?"

"You'll have to ask her that."

"If I can get to see her. I've called her, knocked on her door. She won't speak to me."

Caro said nothing, looking past him at the door. Lucas turned his head. "Jack?"

The older man seated himself beside his wife. "Hello, Lucas. My daughter giving you hell?"

"Something like that."

"She's at home now. Will you go over and see her?"

"What's the point when she won't open the door? Why are you encouraging me? You were the one who wanted me to stay away."

"I think I was wrong. Harriet is different when you're around. Natural. Happier."

"That's hard to believe."

"When you've come as close to death as she did it's bound to change you. But it was like that before the accident too."

"That's different. She had a perfect life. She was perfect."

The couple shared a look that puzzled him. Caro spoke, resting her hand on her husband's knee. "Harriet almost gave up. In the hospital. She didn't want to live."

"Because her life wasn't going to be perfect?"

"No. There was another reason. I think you need to talk to her about that."

"All the same, I can't see why she would just give up. It doesn't sound like her." *She gave up on us.* He pushed the thought away. "All right, I'll speak to her."

"It won't be easy. Harriet has always been good at putting on a front. The way she is, always busy, always volunteering. She's spent her whole life trying to justify her existence."

"That makes no sense. She's your only child and you dote on her."

Jack stood abruptly and went to the bookshelf. He sat back down, a large photo album on his lap.

Curbing his impatience, Lucas watched him leaf through the pages. Finally, he nodded, passing over the book. "I think this will explain a lot."

Lucas took the album, resting it on his lap. There were two photographs, studio portraits, one on each page. On the left, the photo of a boy in his teens. With a sudden surge of recollection, he remembered Angela mentioning something about a boy, but it hadn't registered at the time what it meant. The hair colour was unknown, the bare scalp smooth and shining, but his eyes were Harriet's eyes, a deep blue that would turn to violet. There was a translucent quality to the face. A face that had known suffering. Like Harriet. No wonder Caro was a nervous wreck. To lose one child was bad enough. To almost lose two...

He turned his attention to the other photograph. "This is Harriet?"

Caro answered. Jack sat silent, staring blankly at the photo album. "She was six when this was taken. Her brother was fifteen."

A serious child, with eyes that spoke of a knowledge beyond her years.

"Harriet never mentioned she had a brother. What was his name?"

"Jordy...Jordan. She never speaks of him. Our fault. We should have spoken to her about him. At the time he died it was too painful. After that we didn't know how."

"I still don't understand."

"We never planned on any more children after Jordan. But then he developed leukaemia. We needed a donor."

"So, you had another child. Harriet?"

"Yes. There was a one in four chance of a perfect match. She didn't quite match. But she was our best hope. Unfortunately, he developed chronic graft versus host disease. It attacked his organs. We were trying to get him strong enough for a kidney transplant when he died."

"Was Harriet to be the donor?" Suddenly, those snide remarks to her parents made sense. That almost hidden resentment. It explained her obsession about being wanted for herself. It also explained her quest for perfection.

Caro looked desperately at Jack.

"Yes." Jack's voice was gravelly. "Yes. We are the sort of parents who would ask that of an eight-year-old girl."

"You put your son's life on her shoulders." The rage in his gut burned at the injustice of it. "She was a child."

"It wasn't meant to be that way. We told her it wasn't her fault he died. She seemed to accept that. But ever since she's been trying so hard to be the perfect child. As if she's trying to make up for Jordan."

Lucas remained silent for several minutes.

Finally, he looked up at the older couple. "I need to tell you something."

He sucked in a breath, aware that they wouldn't approve.

"Harriet and I were married the day of the accident."

"That's impossible." Caro's voice held hurt as much as outrage.

"She was eighteen. We were going to tell you the next day, but the accident changed everything."

"Why? Why would she do that?"

"She wanted to come to the U.S. with me. I wanted her to come. We thought…she said it would be the only way. That you would accept a marriage and honour it."

Jack spoke slowly. "You were right. We would never have sanctioned her travelling with you without marriage. Aside from that, your scholarship wouldn't have supported both of you."

"Harriet intended to work. Her ballet teacher had a colleague in Santa Monica who agreed to employ her as a teaching assistant. She had the RADS qualifications. It would have been good experience and it would only have been twelve months."

"But she changed her mind."

"Yes. Understandable, don't you think? With no job and knowing she wouldn't have your support. Knowing how much you would disapprove. I'm surprised she didn't tell you. Because of the legal issues."

"No. She let us assume that she never intended to go with you. It was only recently the possibility was mentioned. When you turned up again."

"A lot of assumptions. She probably assumed I'd deal with the divorce myself. I said I would, when she told me she wouldn't be coming."

Jack nodded wearily. "I don't know what she was thinking. She didn't tell us anything. And there were other complications."

"Which were?"

"Under the circumstances that is really a matter for you and Harriet."

"So, you agree it has to be sorted out?"

"Yes. If you can fix this with Harriet, you would have my eternal gratitude." As they all stood, Jack extended his hand. "From now on you can count on our full cooperation."

"Thank you."

The older man tightened his grip. "You might want to keep in mind that the only times Harriet ever went against us, did something she knew would go against our wishes, were to be with you."

Lucas nodded. "I'm counting on it."

He turned to leave, and Caro stopped him. "Wait. I have something for you."

She left the room, returning with what looked like a shoe box, decorated with teddies. "Harriet made it. Occupational Therapy while she was in the hospital. She kept her personal things in it."

"Why do you have it?"

Again, that look between husband and wife. "We... confiscated it. She was brooding, and we thought it might help. It seemed to. She never mentioned it, or you, again."

"And you thought that was a good thing."

"You weren't around."

"No, I wasn't. That's the first thing I'm going to change. After all that's gone on, you probably find it hard to believe, but I love your daughter. I always have."

**11**

———

There was no answer to his knock. Lucas used the card Jack gave him. It would either stay in Lucas' possession, or be returned to Harriet. It all depended on what happened tonight. Either way, her parents had agreed to step back. They couldn't continue to use emotional blackmail to keep control of their daughter. It had been hard for Caro, but Jack had made the commitment and she had agreed. Finally. If nothing else, he could do that for Harriet.

The apartment was in darkness as Lucas let himself in. The small beep as he operated the card entry sounded loud in the silence, but no response came from inside. He stood still for a few moments to allow his eyes to adjust. Down the hallway, a faint light showed under the door of the master suite. Harriet had been asleep when Jack left, but that meant nothing. She could have fallen asleep with the small lamp beside the bed switched on. It wouldn't be the first time.

Adjusting the box under his arm, he eased the door open and stepped inside. Harriet lay sprawled on her side, the curve of her stomach resting on a pillow, her legs with the braces outlined under the thin sheet. One arm lay protectively over the bump. Her bump, his baby. Their baby. He forced back the rush of emotion that choked his throat. There would be time for that later. There were fences to mend first.

He placed the box on the bedside table and squatted beside the bed. Apart from that glimpse at the office, he hadn't seen her for six months and he wanted to drink her in. Touch her. He clenched his fists and rested his elbows on the edge of the bed, careful not to disturb her.

The hair was different, a short, ragged cut that stood like a halo around the pale face. Her lids and the delicate skin under her eyes seemed bruised, blue veins under translucent skin, gold tipped lashes fanning across her cheek. Her mouth...he sucked in an unwary breath. Slightly parted, the lower lip shone with moisture, as if she'd licked it.

Controlling his impulse to wake her, he sat in the armchair, the box on his lap. Who knew the secrets of a woman's heart? *Why Teddy Bears?* Jack's words echoed in his mind.

*"Doomed to repeat your mistakes."* Standing the lid against the side of the chair, he delved into the box. Something soft wrapped in tissue paper, some photographs, an envelope and a small jeweller's box. He picked up the photographs first, flicking through them, trying not to let the memories distract him.

They were all memories, because they were all of him, apart from one of the pair of them together. He had the same one. The last photograph taken of them together. The last photo taken of Harriet standing, graceful and strong.

The white lacy dress she wore for the wedding ceremony and the graduation dinner afterwards made her look more ethereal than ever. A stranger had offered to take the photo with Harriet's phone and she'd sent it through to his email straight away. Odd that she had a print of it. Hours later, the accident had ended everything, the dress torn and bloody, smeared with grease.

Shoving the photographs away, he picked up the small velvet box. Another memory. The slender ring with intertwined rose-gold vines and diamond and sapphire chips resembling leaves had been a big expense for a student. He'd sold his old desktop computer to pay for it. A pretty thing. He could afford so much more now. All the same, he'd not expected to see it again. He pulled it from the slot, tugging as it snagged. His stomach roiled at the sight of the twisted metal where it had been cut from Harriet's finger.

It brought back the smell of blood and oil and hot metal. Holding Harriet's hand, slimy with his blood and hers as they waited for the rescue services to remove the weight of a black Ducati motorbike from her crushed legs. They'd dragged him away when he tried to lift it off. Warned him of the dangers of her bleeding out if it were removed too soon. Before they were ready with the right equipment.

He could recall the bleak faces of the Paramedics as they spoke among themselves, ready to leap into action once the heavy machine was removed, releasing compressed arteries and veins. Harriet's expression. Resigned. Almost peaceful, as if she half expected this ending. Never believing she deserved more. He hadn't understood at the time. Hadn't suspected that weakness, that vulnerability.

He clenched the ring in his hand, grateful for the pain of the sharp metal. Grimly he put the bauble in his inside jacket pocket with the envelope holding the marriage certificate. If Harriet wouldn't or couldn't fight for their future, he would have to do it for her. His conversation with her parents was only the first skirmish.

The tissue paper separated easily, and something fell to the floor. A soft knitted thing and a photograph that lay face down. He scooped the woollen trifle up and examined it. A baby booty, to go with the other one still on the tissue paper. Along with a knitted bonnet and a half-knitted shawl, the needles still attached. A spiral of queasiness crawled up his abdomen, tightening his gut. The complication. And the Teddies. His heart pounding, he reached for the photograph.

He had no idea how long he stared at the photograph. Harriet's sleepy voice brought him back. "Lucas? How the hell did you get in?"

"Your father gave me a key card."

"He had no right to do that. What are you doing here?" The sheet billowed as she flicked it to one side, revealing her legs, the black knee braces stark in the dim light as she sat up.

"We need to talk. You have something to tell me, I think."

She flushed, one arm moving across her stomach. "What happened to the card I gave you?"

"I still have it."

She was silent for the moment. "Why didn't you use it to get in the other time."

"I didn't use it because you were on the other side of the door saying no."

"But it's all right to sneak in while I'm asleep?" Her tone was chilly. "Give me back the cards. Both of them."

He lay them on the bedside table. "You have a choice. If

you ask me to go, I'll leave. I did consult a lawyer and he said I was entitled." He indicated her stomach. "Think about it."

"A lawyer?"

"Your father. Which brings me to another question. Why did you never tell your father about our plans? About what we'd done that day. You said you would."

"I didn't want him to know how badly I'd stuffed up."

"But they must have known we'd slept together."

She blushed, the colour blending with the pink night shirt. "Why do you say that?"

The numbness seeped away, leaving a deep-seated anger along with the knot in his gut. He'd almost been a father once before and he'd never known. And now she was keeping another child from him.

"Tell me about our baby."

Her hand went to her stomach. but he held the photograph into the light.

"This one Harriet. You make a habit of keeping secrets. Secrets and lies are what define our relationship."

"Faye..." The whispered word told him so many things. She moved away from the lamp, leaving her face in darkness, like his own.

"You called her Faye... It was a little girl?"

"Yes. She was so beautiful, Lucas, but she never had a chance."

"Tell me. Tell me everything. I thought you were protected."

"I was...then. But with the accident I didn't take them that night, or afterwards. No one knew I was on medication. You only have to miss a couple at the right time."

"When did you find out?"

"Not for months. It was a miracle I even fell pregnant in the middle of everything else."

"It went wrong?"

"Not the pregnancy." Her hand trailed along the silver scar, spotlighted by the lamp. "It was the aneurism. I bled out and it affected her...the baby. I went into labour, but she died before she was born. She was six months along but..."

He looked down at the photograph. Harriet, with her hair in a short halo around her head, gazing at the pale perfect features of the tiny baby in her arms. His gut ached, but he had to stay focused. When they were united in reality, they could grieve together.

"Why did they take a photograph?"

"They do that these days. Let you nurse them. They say it helps with the grieving process."

"Did it help?" The picture in his mind was getting clearer.

"I don't know. Maybe. I never cried. I wanted to, but the tears wouldn't come. For a while I wished I died too. I should have been able to save her."

"You can't always save the people you love."

"But..."

"But what?"

"Nothing."

"Do not lie to me." It came out softly. Gently. He didn't want to spook her now. "Harriet. Only the truth can work between us."

"There is no us."

"You can say that with our child in your belly and another child in our history? There is no going back from this Harriet. The day you willingly slept with me, knowing you could fall pregnant, you sealed our fate. I've walked away from you twice at your behest. No matter what you say, I will not walk away from you, or our child again."

Silence. Only the faint rustle as her fingers tangled with

the sheet, twisting it into a coil and releasing it. He waited for her response. It came on the heels of a sigh. "Does what I want matter?"

"It matters."

"What happens if it happens again? If there is no baby?"

"Is that likely?"

"We're over the six months. The obstetrician says the baby is healthy."

"Tick that one off."

"You don't want to live like this. Limited. You travel at the drop of a hat. I can't do that. Not now. I'm not allowed to travel. You spent the last few months overseas. What kind of relationship is that with you living on the other side of the world for months at a time?"

Her resistance stirred something in his chest. Did she realise she was fighting for a real relationship? "We work it out. You won't be pregnant forever. You've never given me a chance to prove myself. As a husband, as a father. I'm demanding that right. It is my right as the father of your child. You know it."

He adjusted the light so he could see her face. "It's time you acknowledged that I do have rights. Rights and obligations. You're trying to deny both if you keep me out of your life and the life of our child. Isn't it about time you met some of your obligations?"

"You sent the divorce papers."

"You know I wouldn't have if you'd told me about the baby."

Her hand clutched the sheets, knuckles white under the light. "You should have been a lawyer. What do you want?"

"Six months. Let me prove myself. If you can't trust me after that time, we'll look at it again."

"You sound so confident. What about your trust? In your view, I've done nothing but lie. What chance do I have of you trusting me?"

"You have to earn it. No more lies. No more evasions. If you're in pain, I want to know. If I do something wrong, you tell me. If I ask a question, you answer me, with the truth."

Harriet stared at Lucas. She should be angry at his demands. Instead there was a warmth in her chest. Six months. A gamble on the future. From the grim expression on his face he intended to enforce it. He said he wouldn't walk away. Not from his child. But would he walk away from her in the end? The next three months would certainly test his resolve. Did he have any idea what it would involve?

"I'm not supposed to bear any weight."

He stood abruptly and sat on the bed, steadying himself with one hand. "Tell me what that means."

"I can't stand on my legs. I have to be assisted with everything. Like when I injured my knee."

"How are you managing?"

"Mum comes over at night to help me shower and Dad comes in the morning to get me out of bed into the wheelchair."

"And in between?"

"I manage. They want me to move back home. They don't want me to live alone."

"I think I've solved that problem."

"How? They'll never stop nagging until I give in."

"I'm moving in."

"You? Moving in?"

"Only until my house is ready for occupancy. Another three weeks and you'll be moving in with me."

"Why? The doctor said I shouldn't lie on my back. And you won't be able to lift me either. I'm not so stupid I'm going to give up my home so I can watch you come and go with all your women."

She edged back as he leaned closer, his expression intimidating. "We will deal with this, right here, right now."

"We will?" Her voice came out squeaky and she wished somebody would kill her already.

He didn't seem to notice, his hands coming up to frame her face, cool on her flushed cheeks. His eyes bored into hers, the green vivid with the intensity of his emotion. "I have never, and I repeat never, cheated on you."

"Never?" It came out in a strained whisper as he rested his forehead against her brow, his warm breath mingling with hers, tasting of coffee.

"Never. Not once. Angela was a colleague. I did her a favour, so you can get that idea out of your mind. I'm not some animal who can't control his libido. If we can't have sex while you're pregnant, we live with it. Or we adapt. There are other ways to reach orgasm. As you should recall. Very pleasurable ways. Would you like me to demonstrate?"

She shook her head. Her heart palpitating in a way it shouldn't be able to do.

"Another time, perhaps?"

What could she say to that? *Freaking hallelujah but pity about the sex?*

Apparently, a response wasn't necessary. He moved away, packing up the contents of her box. She saw him put the small velvet ring case away with a sudden choking feeling. Had he even looked inside?

"Can I have the teddy box?"

He turned sharply, black brows forming a vee of surprise. "Of course. It's your property. Your mother handed it to me this evening before I came."

"You spoke to them? What about?"

"You."

Well, duh. "I know it doesn't look like it, but I'm an adult. I make my own decisions. A long time ago I learned that even well-intentioned people don't know what's best for someone else."

"Yet you did exactly the same when it came to the important things."

"What do you mean?"

"When it came to us, you made a unilateral decision without ever consulting me. From now on, no more decisions that affect both of us without consulting each other."

"This from a man who just informed me I was moving into his house, whether I liked it or not."

"But you did like it. In fact, you told me you loved it. It's beside the point. As of tomorrow, my housekeeper, Mrs. MacAlistair, will be coming in while I'm at work. She's a fully trained nurse and when the baby's born, will be able to assist you."

"There you go again. Walking all over me again. What if I don't like her? Can I fire her?"

"I wouldn't suggest you try it. She's the best housekeeper I've had."

"You would choose your housekeeper over my wishes?"

He actually had the effrontery to laugh. "Don't you know? Housekeepers are far less expendable than...lovers..."

"What about wives?"

The beautiful mouth quirked into a mocking smile. "What about wives?"

"If I could walk. Which incidentally I can't. I would come over there and smack that smirk off your face."

"Are we working up to a pity party?"

"No. How dare you suggest…" She stumbled to a halt as he thrust his face close to hers, kneeling on the bed.

"So, the mountain must come to you…Smack away."

"Don't you dare make me laugh. Don't you dare…" It was too much. The laughter defeated her. Her stomach ached from it, her jaw felt tender to the touch. And the culprit just sat there on his haunches with a smile on his face.

"Feel better now?"

"No."

"They say laughter is the best medicine."

"My stomach hurts and my face hurts. Maybe I overdosed."

"Too much of a good thing? We'll have to break you in gently."

She stared at him, bewildered. "When I was talking to your tech team, they told me you had no sense of humour. I didn't believe them, but they assured me it was true."

"Maybe I haven't had much to laugh about. Computers may be the subject of internet humour but there's not much to laugh about in scripting millions of lines of code." His smile curled downwards. "Or maybe the simple truth is, I was the Laurel to your Hardy. Every comedian needs a straight man."

Her eyes prickled, and she shut them tightly. When she opened them, he was looking down at his hands, lying limply on his knees. His lashes shadowed his eyes and the dim lamplight burnt harsh lines around his mouth hiding the dimple. "Oh…"

His head jerked up at her exclamation and she recognised the emotion in the brief glimpse before his eyes became shuttered. The pain behind the grimness, behind the laughter. But she'd seen something earlier, just as important, and almost missed it. Not when he'd been laughing. It had been her laughter that brought out the dimple for one brief moment in time.

"Lucas." She reached for his hands, twining her fingers through his, palm to palm. What could she say that wasn't inadequate? "I'm so sorry."

Lucas hadn't expected the nerves to hit him in the gut. He was regretting the bacon and eggs already. Harriet sat slightly forward on the seat, looking for her first glimpse of the house in over six months. The last few weeks had gone well. Better than expected. He'd slept in her bed, with her curled up against his back. That way her braces didn't cause problems by digging into his legs. Her stomach made other positions awkward.

It had taken a few nights to get that sorted. Sometimes he could feel the baby kick against his kidneys. Just a flutter of movement, hardly registered before it was gone again. It made it real. Sometimes he deliberately stayed awake in the hope of feeling that small connection with his child.

He'd given in about the housekeeper. Harriet had been so frustrated at his high handedness, he'd decided a few weeks wouldn't matter. She had a cleaner in a couple of times a week and her mother promised to pop by for any personal things. Today was crunch time. The house, everything.

It would have been nicer later, in the spring. The Jacarandas looked stark and bare at this time of year.

"Is this it?" The surprise in her voice was evident. Whether good surprise or bad surprise, he wasn't sure. He pulled in off the street to the new raised carport.

She stared at the freshly painted building. "This is different. I was thinking I'd be getting carried everywhere."

"We can go with that if you prefer."

Her smile lit up his morning. "Maybe sometimes."

Once in the wheelchair she moved onto the veranda, looking at everything. "This is amazing. It's almost like you made it for me." She stopped with a jerk, her face flushing. "That sounds awfully conceited. It's convenient for you too I suppose. No lugging groceries across the yard and up the steps."

"The architect said accessibility made for good resale value." He softened it with a sly smile that told her he'd done it with her in mind.

"And you're all about the dollars." She said it with a grin as she made her way to the front door. "I'm dying to see what you've done inside."

"Not a lot in the bedrooms. Painted and polished but you might like to decide the soft furnishings."

"Trying to turn me into a good little house-frau?"

"I live in hope."

She had no answer to that, speeding off to look at the lounge area. In her thorough way, she scoured the place, open mouthed. "I can't believe it." Her hands stroked the granite bench top in the kitchen. "I can't believe it. This is more than just standard accessibility. You've allowed for a wheelchair." The expression on her face became thoughtful. "You know this dropped bench will be no good for people in electric wheelchairs. It's too low."

The stairs earned him a dirty look. "Have you finished renovating downstairs?"

"Sure. You want to go down and see what's been done."

"Will you take me down?"

"You can take yourself. Check out the glass door on the other side of the stairs."

Her squeal of delight eased some of the tension and he jogged down the stairs to wait for her. The slow lift must have given her time to think because the subdued Harriet that emerged brought the nerves back again.

"Why did you do it, Lucas?"

He demanded truth from her. No evasions.

"I had the plans drawn up last year, while we were going out together."

"You were planning this back then?"

"I bought the house when I first came back to Australia with settling down in mind. I...hoped with you. It took longer than I expected to find you."

"We'd all moved."

"Yes."

"You didn't know then about the wheelchair."

"I thought of selling. Getting something on flat ground, but that's not as easy as it looks in Brisbane. Especially close to the city."

Hunching her shoulders, she studied her hands. "I thought you hated me back then."

"You were right. But I still wanted you."

"When did it change?"

"The hating lasted about five minutes. The wanting never stopped"

"Even before you knew."

"I think I was lost the moment I heard you laugh. I was jealous of Jimmie because you were his friend."

"Poor Jimmie."

"Lucky Jimmie, to be working with you all this time."

"He's not that keen on basketball you know. He prefers movies."

"Poor Jimmie, in that case. You were using him."

"I never expected him to invite you along. Now, you're best buddies." She waved a hand at the entertainment area. "He'll expect an invite to the barbeques."

"If you're trying to put me off it isn't working. I like him."

She shook her head. "You win."

"I always win."

The smile was small, but he caught it.

"You're delusional, Lucas Hall. Show me the pool and then I want to see where I sleep."

"As you wish, M'lady."

The bed was the same, the purple velvet with the mounds of cushions. She glanced over at Lucas, knowing he was thinking about the same things. The smirk had to go. He looked far too smug. "You need to get rid of some of these cushions."

"Don't you like them?" He sounded wounded but there was a spark in his eye.

"What's that saying, 'All things in moderation'? There is nothing moderate about that pile of cushions.

"What do you suggest I do with them?"

With a shrug, she headed for the en-suite bathroom. "The doghouse?"

"And me with them?" There was definitely a wicked lilt to his voice.

"If the shoe fits."

"I have exceptionally large feet."

"Boasting ill becomes you."

"Drama Queen."

He followed her into the bathroom. Which would have mattered once, but like the Tardis, there was a lot more room inside than appeared on the outside. If the Tardis had been lined with white marble tiles and fitted with polished brass lever taps and support rails.

"It's lucky I'm a well brought up young lady or I would have said a really nasty word."

"What's wrong with it? I made it just how you like it."

"It's big. I mean ginormous big. Where did the space come from?"

"There was a funny back corner office. Knock down one wall and hey presto. It didn't get any light and I prefer my office closer to the kitchen."

"Always hungry."

"You know me so well."

"I know for sure this is going to amuse you. Junior is pressing on my bladder."

With an enthusiasm that was a little wearing, he had her on the pedestal in no time flat. "You can leave now."

He looked down his long nose, with brows raised until she could have throttled him. Or kissed him. Or both. Just as well she wasn't into erotic asphyxiation.

"This is about the, seeing you pee isn't romantic thing, isn't it?"

She dragged her mind back from a vision of Lucas Hall splayed naked on the bed apart from her favourite emerald green scarf around his throat. "Romance. Not happening here. Go."

He was waiting right outside and could probably hear every last tinkle. She was sort of getting used to it after all these weeks. Come Monday when his housekeeper returned, he'd probably abdicate the responsibility and find himself at the other end of this mansion when she needed to go.

He did leave her alone when she was back in her wheelchair, muttering something about the meal. Even the walk-in robe was big enough to throw a party in. All her clothes were neatly hung on the low rails or folded onto easily accessible shelves. If a man could write an encryption program in hot demand by the leaders of the free world, he better be able to design a walk-in-robe. Or presumably instruct the renovator on what he wanted.

Sitting on the veranda, she reluctantly admitted he was winning her over. But it was only three weeks. Holidays don't last that long and everything is a novelty. Now she was in his house it would be interesting to see how he handled it.

A low rumble of sound drew her attention to the garden. She'd noticed the mix of herbal scents as soon as she got out of the car. The whole front yard appeared to be devoted to herbs. Lucas moved around gathering bits and pieces. She recognised rosemary and something that looked like basil. If basil grew in the winter? It didn't surprise her. He always used herbs in cooking, a legacy of his Italian grandmother. The weirdest thing was the humming. No-one could ever call him musical.

The sound stopped as he caught sight of her, elbows on the low rail of the veranda. "Would you like a posy?"

"What do you have?"

"I've got something for everything. Lavender?"

"Lovely."

"If I remembered my Shakespeare I could stand here and quote the balcony scene."

"You can remember forty zillion lines of code and can't remember some of the most romantic lines in literature. Couldn't you at least try? After all, you said you've been practicing conversation."

"I've been watching a lot of cable in the U.S. as well. Oh well, here goes." He struck a pose, one arm outstretched with a handful of leaves and the other on his heart. "But soft, what light though yonder window breaks. It is the East and Harriet is the sun." He stopped, laughter in his eyes. "Sorry, that's all I've got."

"It's enough." She blew him a smiling kiss and turned away, afraid to let him see how much he affected her.

Later that night, she wrapped her arm around his waist, listening to his regular breathing. He'd given her such a shock that evening in the shower she hadn't known where to look. She expected him to leave once he settled her on the shower seat. When he'd unzipped and wandered over to the pedestal, she'd thought he was joking, until the sound of him urinating made it clear it wasn't.

"Is that supposed to be funny?"

"No. It's a solution to a dangerous problem."

"How does that work?"

He'd sauntered back to lean on the wall by the shower, zipping up his fly as he came and washing his hands in the spray from the shower. Watching as she scrubbed. And not in a clinical way.

"It's like this. I saw how you looked at me this afternoon after I did that romantic Shakespeare thing. You were ready to jump over the balcony and do me in the tansy."

"How do you manage to make that sound even dirtier than it should be?"

"Natural talent."

"I still don't see how going to the bathroom with me in

the same room is going to solve my...my uncontrollable lust for your...poetry."

"Simple. You said seeing someone peeing makes them unromantic. Problem solved. I'm now totally unromantic. You can look at me, probably even totally naked, and all you would think is, I saw him pee in the bathroom. Not interesting."

Totally naked. For a math genius he was great at painting pictures. "I think I'm going for the throttling."

"Is that before or after?"

"Before or after what?"

"Kissing me." He grinned lasciviously.

It was getting harder and harder not to laugh at him. "Are you reading my mind?"

"I hope so, if it involves kissing."

"There's no point."

"You do remember there are other positions apart from missionary? You don't have to have sex lying on your back."

All sorts of erotic images raced across her mind, like a slide show of flesh tinted statuary. Mentally she crossed off anything that required kneeling. It still left some tantalising possibilities. Lucas never minded trying something new out in the past. He could laugh his way through the most awkward positions and still make her feel good.

He leaned over and pinched her nipples already beading with arousal. "I take it the whole peeing thing didn't work."

"Mentioning it is extremely unromantic."

"I suppose pure unadulterated lust has nothing to do with romance. So, we've just proven the whole argument flawed."

"If that's your idea of scientific method, I'm surprised your program didn't blow up the Pentagon."

"If that's what I wanted it to do, it would have. But I'm a peaceable man. I prefer to make love, not war."

"I'm quite interested. Can you show me some empiric data to support that statement?"

"It would be my pleasure."

## 12

The birthing centre was supposed to be state of the art, but it wasn't like any hospital he'd been inside. It was all pale pinks and carpets and looked more like a very lush private hotel. Harriet and her midwife were wallowing in a Jacuzzi which only increased his disorientation.

The water-birth had been organised while he was away, and while he understood in theory this would be easier on Harriet, the thought of her giving birth underwater kind of creeped him out. The long list of qualifications held by the nursing sister reassured him, along with the knowledge her obstetrician was in the building.

"Are you ready, Dad?" A woman in her forties calling him dad was also kind of creepy but her easy competence shone through.

This was for Harriet and their baby. With a deep breath, he stepped into the water, manoeuvring behind her so he could support her when she started to push. He was wearing swim shorts and Harriet had started off with a loose t-shirt that had been discarded now she was so close, leaving her in just a sports bra. It shouldn't have been sexy, but he had to focus his mind on what was happening. Their baby was about to change everything.

The midwife was totally focused. "Anytime now, Harriet."

Afterwards he hardly remembered the details. Harriet panting, a rush of pink fluid in the water and then the baby. It all seemed too easy until he looked at the clock and realised how much time had passed.

Her joyful glow, despite her weariness as their son was placed in her arms, triggered a swell of emotion he could barely contain. His Harriet was so strong. She didn't think so, but he could see it every day. He forced back the moisture in his eyes, aware of the other people in the room.

Harriet looked up at him with her unique radiance and smiled. "It's all right."

As if she knew the tangle of feelings that wrenched his insides. She did of course. She always had been in tune with him in the past, making her defection incomprehensible.

"Thank you, Lucas. Thank you for our little boy."

He couldn't think of anything to say that wouldn't come out tied up in knots, but she nodded and held out the baby. "What will we call him?"

They'd talked about it, mooting several names, but there was really only one answer for a child so much like Harriet, so like her brother. "Jordan."

Her eyes widened. "How did you know?"

"Your parents told me."

"And you're all right with it? You don't think it's morbid?"

"I think it's right. We can use one of the other names as well." Her hand on his arm squeezed tight. The nerves coiled in his stomach eased. He hoped this would help her at least talk to her parents about her brother. He snorted.

The irony of Lucas Hall trying to mend someone like Harriet when he was a total screw up. Physician heal thyself. Not Shakespeare this time. Maybe the bible. He was getting to be a regular Mr. Fixit.

The baby stirred in his arms, lavender eyes unfocused. "Hello, Jordan Hall."

The wave of love that swept over him, the urge to protect this tiny being, it was almost too much. The stakes were too high for him to sit back and hope for the best. With Jordan's birth, they just got higher. And the shadow in Harriet's eyes as she looked at her baby was just one more warning not to slacken his vigilance.

Lucas adjusted the sheet across Jordan's chest under Harriet's watchful gaze. "He's grown so much." Tomorrow, he had to return to work. He'd taken three weeks off after the birth and loved the time bonding with the baby. And with Harriet.

She stroked the baby's quiff of blonde hair with gentle fingers before moving away from the cot and into their bedroom. "I'm glad he is a boy. I wouldn't like to feel I was replacing Faye."

Lucas lifted her onto the bed and sat beside her. She'd been quiet all evening, meditating on the past, he suspected. He tightened his grip around her shoulders. "I'm sorry I wasn't here for you. I'm sorry I never had the chance to hold our first baby."

"When they told me she'd died, I think that was the moment I realised how empty my life was going to be. Until then I thought I would have a part of you with my baby." She burrowed into his shoulder. "I didn't want to go on. It nearly broke Mum and Dad's heart. When I saw what I was doing to them, after everything, after Jordan. I was so ashamed."

"Don't ever be ashamed. You were grieving. For more than just our lost baby."

She trembled against him and finally they came, the long shuddering sobs she'd held inside for over seven long years. He wrapped himself around her, rocking her as the tears fell, dampening his shirt. His own tears etched their way down his cheeks forming droplets on the spiked strands of blond hair under his chin. After a while he thought she slept, her breathing soft and even. He held her close, determined she would never feel alone again.

He knew that aching loneliness first hand, but he'd come late to the loss of the child he'd never known, too long ago to have the sharp edge of grief. It could never be real to him, not like Harriet would feel it. Soon, very soon his time would be up. He could only hope and pray he'd done enough, been enough to prove himself to Harry. Because he had too much to lose now. Harry had always been an indelible mark on his heart. He could rip it out, bury it deep and still live, but now she'd become his soul and if she ever took that away, he would die inside.

A soft grizzle from the nursery told him the other resident of his heart would soon be wide awake. Gently, he lay Harriet down, smiling at her small murmur of protest. There was time enough to show her, within the constraints of the doctor's recommendation.

Harriet woke to the sound of the shower. Her heart did a happy dance that Lucas was home after a trip that had extended way longer than expected, but her head wanted to punish him a little for making her worry.

He appeared at the bathroom door, still rubbing at his wet hair with a towel. Wearing nothing else. She sucked in a harsh breath and clenched her toes.

Casually tossing the towel into the hamper, he fixed his gaze on her hopefully stern face. "Am I in the doghouse?"

"With a gazillion purple cushions to keep you company? You should be so lucky. You almost missed the party. The one you insisted on having."

"I'm sorry, Harry." He kissed her shoulder and the nape of her neck. She kind of liked the shorter hairstyle. Practical with a baby but it had other advantages.

"Crawling will be required. Lots of crawling."

"You are so demanding, woman."

The bedclothes heaved and she giggled as he vanished under them. His fingers wrapped around her toes. "Cold, much."

His "sorry" was muffled as his hands disappeared. She waited as there was a flurry of movement at the foot of the bed and a cool draft touched the soles of her feet. A warm damp kiss landed on the arch of one foot and her toes curled in appreciation. He knew just what to do.

"I missed you."

"Me, or this." His fingers did the talking, skipping over the braces to seek the hot bloom of heat, flicking across the hard nub. She twitched under his touch and he soothed it with his mouth, warm and moist.

She groaned and tilted her hips for more. "This of course."

He chuckled and complied, the flick of his tongue, the thrust of his fingers taking her over the edge into bliss.

·  ·  ·

She sighed as she came down to earth, snuggling into his shoulder when he moved to hold her. "I was all ready to give you a hard time for being late home but now I'm feeling all mellow."

"Now I know how to get around you. One orgasm and I'm home and hosed."

"I don't know about this 'one', business. I did mention lots of crawling. That implies a multiple quantity. Perhaps one for every day you were late."

"Three days, three orgasms. Sounds fair to me."

"That's not counting the one you just gave me. We'll assume that was a freebie. A Sample. A trial download."

"I should have you negotiating my military contracts. You wouldn't let them get away with anything."

"Well, on careful consideration maybe I missed you too. You realise you have to crawl to Mrs. Mac too."

His response was prompt. "I'll send her flowers."

"She'll love that."

He propped himself up on his elbow and looked down at her with a strange expression. "You've changed."

"In what way?"

"Bossier. But in a good way. I like it."

She thought about it for a moment. Trying to remember. "I argued with you right from the start."

"It's different. You were pushing me away. Now...it's different. It feels different."

"I'm not pushing you away?"

"Demanding three orgasms with one on credit isn't exactly pushing me away."

"I suppose not." His eyes ate her up, tender yet simmering with desire. It warmed her chest, bubbled up into laughter. "What have you done to me? Turned me into a sex-addict?"

Growling, he nipped her shoulder and down lower, suckling her nipple. "I'm going to have to work out a way to keep you with me."

"I don't think you'll have to try too hard."

He looked up at her, a half smile curling his mouth, his luscious beautiful mouth that did so many wonderful things. "I was actually thinking about something else..." Sitting up abruptly, he gripped her wrist. "Do you mean that?"

Disarmed by his serious tone, she nodded. Something changed. Whether it was the suppressed excitement radiating from Lucas, or her own conviction that this was a key moment. A life-changing moment.

"Don't move a muscle. I'll be right back."

Taking the spirit rather than the words themselves, Harriet sat up, smoothing the covers and tucking them around her chest. Something in his eyes as he'd made the demand left her feeling vulnerable, exposed. She hadn't felt that way in a long time. Which was odd, because she'd spent so long, years, keeping up the façade to hide it. *When had it changed?* It had to be Lucas. When he was with her, she was real. He'd broken her down without her even noticing.

There'd been moments. The birth of Jordy. The night they cried together over lost Faye. The long talk she'd had with her parents about her childhood, about Jordan. She could think about her brother without that sensation of falling, of failing to hold on tight enough. Like Faye.

She glanced over at the wall where the photograph of baby Jordan hung, alongside an enlargement of the photograph of herself with tiny Faye. Lucas had taken the one of Jordy to be framed and come back with both. She could look at it now without that hollow feeling. Only a sense of gratitude for the comfort she'd felt with the child inside her in the lonely months after she'd sent Lucas away.

The air of suppressed excitement still hung about him as he flopped back on the bed beside her, tucking one leg under him so he could sit closely. Computer geek or not, he had the body of a god. He batted her hand away from his abs. "Not now. Later."

His fist uncurled on her lap and she stared down at the glint of blue and gold and the flash of diamonds. Wonderingly she touched it with her finger, almost afraid it would vanish. "You had it mended."

"It's been six months. I asked for six months to prove myself. Will you wear my ring again?"

She pulled back her hand and saw him flinch. "Wait. That's not my answer. I need to know." She licked dry lips. "What about me? Did I pass?"

"No more lies? You tell me."

"No lies. Only truth. I love you, Lucas. So much."

"Then you pass."

"Yes. The answer is yes."

She reached out for the ring and his fist closed. "Not now. Tonight. This time we do it right."

"At the party?"

"Yes. With your parents and our friends."

"It seems a long time away." She looked up at him coyly and laughed when his eyes darkened. "Is it later, yet?"

Much later, Harriet looked around the spacious living room. Not a big crowd. Her parents, some friends of Lucas, Graeme, Jimmie. Angela and a disreputable looking giant with a beard and glasses. Not what she expected. Mrs. Mac holding Jordy, wide eyed and alert. Hopefully he would last the distance.

The big surprise was Father O'Connor. He'd retired years ago. She glanced across at Lucas who was talking closely with Jimmie. He turned and caught her gaze. "It's time." He mouthed the words and a rush of butterflies invaded her stomach. *Courage. I has it.* Thanks to Lucas.

She put her hands to the wheels and made her way across the room, careful not to let the long skirt of her purple velvet dress catch. Caro was shushing everyone, waving for them to take a seat. That feeling of exposure hunched her shoulders. "Ready, Harry?"

Looking up she met his eyes, holding everything. Love, tenderness and a smidgen of desire, and something else. Pride. She was so not going to cry. Biting her lip, she let him adjust the chair into position. Father O'Connor pulled out a long strip of fabric and looped it around his neck. "So, this is official?"

Lucas nodded. He tossed down one of the despised purple cushions and knelt in front of her, his hand lightly touching the jewelled flower clips in her hair. "I'm glad you dressed up. Are they the same ones?"

"Yes. The other dress was wrecked in the accident, so I thought this would be appropriate."

"Very appropriate, I fell in love with you in that dress that first night at the party."

A cough from the priest silenced them. Lucas gripped her hands loosely on her lap.

The priest's sonorous voice rolled over her, but she couldn't take her eyes from Lucas. She heard Father welcome the guests. "We are gathered here today, in the presence of friends and family to support Lucas and Harriet Hall as they renew their vows." A flurry of sound interrupted the priest but settled almost immediately. She dared a glance around and saw the eager anticipation in the audience. Her mother's eyes were bright with happy tears, and her father's smile was full of pride.

"Eight years ago, this fine young couple eloped, but as some of you know, an accident on their wedding night broke them apart. Now they have found their way back to each other and are here to recommit to the loving vows they made to each other on their wedding day."

The familiar words came easily, prompted by the priest. To have and to hold, keeping only unto you. Old fashioned vows for an old-fashioned forever love. Her chest wanted to explode with it, warmth enveloping her, swamping her. She stared into the face of the man she'd loved from the moment she'd seen him, seeing all the love he had for her in his expression, open for the world to see.

Jimmie handed Lucas her ring. He looked deep into her eyes as he pushed it over her knuckle. "I love you, Harriet. No matter how hard I tried, I couldn't push you out of my heart. You belong there. This is never coming off again."

Tears came as she smiled at him, her love shining through the sparkling droplets. "They had to cut it off me the first time."

He kissed her hand as he lay it down, so she could take the other ring from their impromptu best man. The plain band with the engraved inscription inside slid home easily. As if it belonged.

"You may kiss the bride."

His lips touched hers, almost tentatively, softening as she responded, putting her heart into the kiss, the tender caress speaking of all they wanted to say. The room erupted around them, but they stayed for those moments in a world of two.

She touched his hand. "You kept your ring too."

"It was never off my finger until the day I saw your name on the funding application."

"Why did you take it off?"

"At first I didn't want you to know. After that, I knew I had to earn the right to wear it again."

"We made things hard for ourselves."

"It's worth it in the long run. Knowing we have what it takes." His fingers traced the length of her fingers to touch the pattern on her wedding ring.

People hovered, waiting to congratulate, to exclaim. She turned her hand to link her fingers in his. "I suppose we have to be social now. Are you feeling up to it?"

"I'm all good. With you beside me I can conquer the world."

"You mean you didn't already?" His fugitive dimple peeped out and she reached over to kiss it. "Welcome back."

*H*arriet stared, forgetting to blink. "It's enormous."

"It's not the size, it's what you do with it."

"Idiot. Why on earth do you need a plane that big?"

"To transport my ever-growing family." Lucas rubbed her swollen tummy with a cheeky grin.

Suddenly anxious, she looked up at his smiling face. "You don't mind? We had planned to wait a while."

"I guess it was a bit unexpected, considering we were supposed to be taking precautions. It's not like I wasn't aware of the risks. It takes two to tango."

"Is that what you call it?"

"The horizontal tango? Of course. The dance of love." He shunted his hips from side to side, his arms in a dance pose and she glanced around the empty tarmac. Only Mrs. Mac and Jordy could see her husband being utterly, adorably ridiculous and they were both too busy admiring the plane. Jordy was gabbling in his inimitable way and the dour Scotswoman watched him with something that almost resembled a smile.

Lucas squatted to bring himself to her eye level. "Now we come to the big question."

"The big question? You expect me to pay for it, Mr. Billionaire, who buys 747's out of his pocket money."

"The question is, will you let me carry you up the stairs, or am I expected to pay more of my hard-earned billions to supply you with elevator access?"

"Oh." Harriet looked over his shoulder at the staircase. She was tempted to insist on using her crutches to get herself up. It would leave her exhausted but assuage her pride. A young man in uniform stood at the top, welcoming Jordy who looked quite smug in the arms of his nanny.

There were more important things than pride. "I suppose if Master Jordan deigns to be carried, as his mother I shouldn't be too proud to accept a lift."

"I can't wait to get you into our bedroom, Mrs. Hall. I think it's time you were inducted into the Mile-High club." He looked into her eyes, seeing the uncertainty. "My induction too, my love. Don't ever forget it."

Recovering her poise, in as much as you could be poised when being carried up a flight of stairs by a hunk of gorgeous manhood, Harriet attempted a regal manner. "Indeed Mr. Hall. I'm gratified you intend to supply me with a bedroom. I understood bathrooms are the usual venue for such things."

"Not just one bedroom, but two. I refuse to share with Mrs. Mac and Jordy." He seated her in one of the luxurious leather armchairs and stood back. "So, what do you think?"

"Whoah." *What on earth could you say?* Empty space, cream leather, walnut cabinets, lush carpet. *Lush cream carpet?* "I hope Jordy doesn't spill his dinner. I hate to think of the cleaning bill."

"Spoilsport. I didn't choose the décor. I hate to admit it

but I'm a bit of a skinflint. I got it second-hand. Some middle eastern potentate was upgrading."

She raised her brows at him. "Cheap at half the price?"

He shrugged. "It takes time to build one of these and I was in a hurry. This had all the specs I was looking for. We can redecorate."

Harriet gazed up at his face, noting the anxious frown. He'd rushed into buying something so he could have them with him straight away. Nothing to complain about in that. "It's fine. I won't be doing the cleaning, after all."

The uniformed attendant appeared with her chair, placing it neatly behind her before fading away discreetly. "It comes with staff?"

"Pilots of course. And two attendants. They work in shifts."

"Why is this plane more luxurious than our house?"

"Because I want you to be comfortable when we travel."

For the first time since they arrived at the airfield, she really looked at him. "You're serious. You really intend us to fly with you."

"Where possible. Once the children are older it won't always be practical. Having so much of my core business in the U.S. and Canada makes it necessary to travel. I need to keep ahead of the trends and that can't be done staying at home."

"You have no intention of letting me be your ball and chain, do you?"

"I don't know about a ball. But I could think of some interesting things to do with a chain."

"Be serious."

"Why should I? You make me happy every moment of every day."

"How unscientific. Shouldn't that be micro-seconds?"

"Don't go overboard. Who wants to be that happy? We need some misery to highlight the happy."

"Why am I not feeling the misery here?"

"Because you've had your share. You are going to be happy every nano-second, pico-second, whatever. This is my personal crusade."

His eyes were suddenly serious, the emerald depths glowing. "You are everything I ever wanted. Everything I ever dreamed. You are my gift from the Elven realms, my heart, my soul, my Faerie Queen. I knew it the day we met."

"How did a geek get to be so poetic?"

"I've been practicing."

"Have I told you lately that I love you?"

"You tell me with your eyes, but the words would be good. It must be, I don't know, hundreds of billions of nano-seconds since you last told me. Thousands."

"You are a genius level, prize idiot. And I love you."

"I know. That's why I'm a genius level prize idiot. Because I almost let you go. Twice"

"Kiss me, Mr. Hall."

"I intend to do more than that."

# ABOUT THE AUTHOR

Fiona M Marsden started out as an avid reader. She was a late starter in finding romance novels, but once found, they became an addiction. Considering she wrote poetry and stories from a young age, it was only logical that the next step would be to write her own romances.

Published Work
    The Runaway Christmas Elf
    Swept Away Hearts of Brizvegas Book 1
    Road Trip Baby Hearts of Brizvegas Book 2
    Man of Ice Hearts of Brizvegas Book 3
    The Forgotten Groomsman Hearts of Brizvegas Book 4
    Coming Soon Hearts of Brizvegas Books 1-4 Anthology

Short Stories
    "The Sunstone Bride", Little Gems Short Story Anthology 2016, RWAus.
    "The Sunstone Inheritance", Little Gems Short Story Anthology 2016, RWAus.
    "Heart of Stone", Little Gems Short Story Anthology 2017.
    "The Jaded Rake", Little Gems Short Story Anthology 2018
    "Club 73", Spicy Bites Short Story Anthology 2018 RWAus
    "Unmasked", Spicy Bites Short Story Anthology 2019

"Tyger Tyger", Little Gems Short Story Anthology 2019
"Tiger Lily", Little Gems Short Story Anthology 2019

www.fionamarsden.com
fiona@fionamarsden.com